# BORDERLINE
# PSYCHOPATHOLOGY
# ——AND ITS TREATMENT——

# BORDERLINE PSYCHOPATHOLOGY
## ——AND ITS TREATMENT——

Gerald Adler, M.D.

New York · JASON ARONSON · London

10 9 8 7 6 5 4 3 2 1

Library of Congress Cataloging in Publication Data
Adler, Gerald, 1930–
    Borderline psychopathology and its treatment.
    Includes bibliographies and index.
    1. Borderline personality disorders.   I. Title.
[DNLM: 1. Mental Disorders—therapy.   2. Psychopathology.
WM 400 A237b]
RC569.5.B67A35   1985        616.89        84-24171
ISBN 0-87668-739-7

Manufactured in the United States of America.

To Corinne
and our children
Andrew, Emily, Jennifer, and Susan

# Contents

*vii*

## PART III
## OTHER TREATMENT ISSUES

# Preface

This book is essentially a synthesis of papers I published—sometimes as co-author with Dan H. Buie—over the past 15 years. The thesis that Buie and I developed to account for borderline psychopathology is a complex one, and was originally presented in two overlapping theoretical papers, the first concentrating on development, the second on psychodynamics. In order to eliminate redundancy, on the one hand, and by way of fleshing out our thesis, on the other, I have chosen here to combine the two papers and expand on some of their theoretical implications in a way that was not possible in journal publication. These two papers, then, form the backbone of Chapters 1 through 4, which present the fullest statement of our theoretical position to date. The remainder of the volume follows essentially the same strategy, combining and expanding upon articles dealing with specific aspects of our understanding that could not be treated in depth in the original two papers. These have mainly to do with treatment issues.

Obviously, many of the ideas in this book have grown out of my almost 20-year collaboration with Dan Buie. This collaboration extended even beyond the co-authorship of scholarly papers to include ongoing informal dialogues about our patients, our reactions to them, and the relationship of our thinking to psychoanalytic clinical and developmental theories, and informs even those papers I authored singly. But since I am recasting many of our ideas in a way that at times may differ slightly in emphasis from our original conceptions, and am elaborating some of those ideas for the sake of clarity, I have chosen here to write in the first-person singular so as best to indicate my ultimate responsibility for them.

If I were asked to characterize my approach in a summary way, I should answer first in the negative: I do not subscribe to the view that "borderline" is a "wastebasket term," a manifestation of our muddled thinking, perhaps an iatrogenic myth based upon our failure to understand some severely vulnerable patients. The problem is not in the mind of the therapist, in other words. But neither do I subscribe to the position on the other extreme, which tends to focus exclusively on objectively observable *behavioral* manifestations of the ambivalence that is said to lie at the root of the disorder. Rather, I take a middle position, giving as much weight to the patient's reports of his *subjective* experience as I do to his behavior in the transference. Indeed, these reports of what the patient feels—his "inner emptiness," his "aloneness"—were the spur and the foundation for my theoretical formulations.

# ————— Acknowledgments —————

Over the years I have profited from the counsel of a number of colleagues: Drs. Michael F. Basch, David A. Berkowitz, Stephen B. Bernstein, Harold N. Boris, Louis S. Chase, Howard A. Corwin, Ralph P. Engle, Jr., Cornelus Heijn, Jr., Robert Jampel, Otto F. Kernberg, Anton O. Kris, Charles E. Magraw, Sterrett Mayson, William W. Meissner, Paul G. Myerson, S. Joseph Nemetz, Paul H. Ornstein, Ana-Maria Rizzuto, Leon N. Shapiro, George E. Vaillant, Douglas Welpton, and Martin Zelin. I am particularly grateful for the editorial help of Nicholas Cariello. His skill has made this book into a synthesis rather than a mere compilation of papers. His ability to stand back and see my work as a whole has helped me clarify its relationship to other contributions to the study of borderline patients.

# BORDERLINE PSYCHOPATHOLOGY
—AND ITS TREATMENT—

# One

# The Primary Basis of Borderline Psychopathology

## Ambivalence or Insufficiency?

Most contemporary accounts of the borderline personality disorder emphasize the quality and organization of introjects as the primary basis of psychopathology. Kernberg (1975), for example, traces the roots of the disorder to the very young infant's inability to integrate self and object representations established under the influence of libidinal drive derivatives with those established under the influence of aggressive drive derivatives. The consequent division of introjects and identifications of contrasting affective coloration (typically, images of an "all-good" mother from images of an "all-bad" mother) is then turned to defensive purposes in order to ward off intense ambivalence conflicts relating to the object (p. 25). Thus, "splitting"—the most prominent of the primitive defenses employed by the borderline patient —"prevent[s] diffusion of anxiety within the ego and pro- tect[s] the positive introjections and identifications" (p. 28) against invasion by aggressive affects. The primitive de- fenses of projection, projective identification, and idealiza- tion may similarly be understood in terms of the need to keep apart "positive" and "negative" introjects, thereby to alleviate or ward off ambivalence conflicts arising from hostile aggressive affects directed toward the "all-good" introject. The contributions of Meissner (1982), Masterson (1976), and Volkan (1976), to name only three, can all be interpreted as following from this theoretical emphasis on developmental failure in synthesizing introjects of contrast- ing affective coloration, and its subsequent defensive use.

I present this view in some detail not only because I believe it to be among the more persuasive and systematic theories of borderline psychopathology, but also—and mainly—to highlight the ways in which my own findings depart from it. Like Kernberg, I believe that the quality and organization of introjects is important in the development and treatment of the borderline disorder, but *at a later point in development and at a later time in treatment* than is generally supposed. Even more crucial to borderline psychopathology, in my view, and even more significant for treatment, is a *functional insufficiency and correlative instability* of certain kinds of introjects and identifications that are needed to sustain the psychological self. *The primary sector of borderline psychopathology, that is, involves a relative developmental failure in formation of introjects that provide to the self a function of holding-soothing security.* Specifically, the formation of holding introjects is quantita- tively inadequate, and those that have formed are unstable, being subject to regressive loss of function in the face of excessive tension arising within the dyadic situation. To a significant degree, then, the borderline patient lacks, *in the first instance*, as well as in consequence of regression, those "positive" introjects whose division from his "negative" introjects (the intrapsychic manifestation of his inability to tolerate ambivalence) is said to determine his psychopathology in the Kernbergian view. He lacks, thereby, adequate internal resources to maintain holding-soothing security in his adult life.

I shall, of course, be elaborating this view in much greater detail in this and subsequent chapters, with particular reference to issues of development, psychodynamics, and treatment. In order to circumscribe my primary concerns in undertaking a study of borderline patients, and by way of describing the features of these patients generally, I should like first to consider the ways in which current theories stressing the quality and organization of introjects—"ambivalence theory"* hereinafter—would conceptualize these same features. This consideration should then serve as a

---

*In introducing the term "ambivalence theory," I mean it to refer in a shorthand way to the idea of divided introjects of contrasting affective coloration. I do *not* mean ambivalence of the sort associated with the higher-level functioning of conflicted individuals in typical dyadic or triadic situations, still less the *conscious* ambivalence of even the healthiest people in everyday dealings with others. Rather, I refer to the idea that the borderline patient keeps apart "positive" and "negative" introjects because he is unable to tolerate ambivalence toward the whole object. I would, of course, prefer the more accurate "inability-to-tolerate-ambivalence theory" were it not so cumbersome. I should add that even borderline patients suffering from insufficiency are prone to feelings of ambivalence toward their primary objects. But the major issue for them remains one of insufficiency.

Let me reiterate, moreover, that I do not deny the usefulness of "ambivalence theory" in understanding the development and treatment of the borderline patient. It plays a crucial role once the primary issue of insufficiency has been resolved (see Chapter 4).

basis for comparison with my own view, which I believe offers a more coherent—for being more complete—account of borderline psychopathology as it is understood today.

## Description of Psychopathology

Most commentators on the borderline disorder see the key to its diagnosis as lying in the patient's vulnerability to stress: Borderline patients are dramatically prone to regress in the areas of ego functioning, object relations, and self-cohesiveness in the face of excessive tension arising within dyadic situations. Even in the nonregressed state, however, specific vulnerabilities in each of these three areas can often be identified.

### EGO FUNCTIONING IN THE NONREGRESSED STATE

In his everyday life, the borderline patient maintains a relatively high level of functioning and adaptation to reality, along with a relatively firm sense of reality, feeling of reality, and testing of reality. He has often established himself in a personally meaningful pursuit, such as education or a profession, that serves as a resource for emotional sustenance and reinforcement of ego integrity. At the same time, however, he typically exhibits some degree of ego instability and weakness, often manifested in a nonspecific diminution of impulse control with a tendency to direct expression of impulses (Meissner 1982, *DSM-III*). He generally feels, moreover, some anxiety of a free-floating but signal type, related qualitatively to separation. These factors, although adequately controlled by higher-order (neurotic) defenses in the nonregressed state, typically play a large part in his subsequent vulnerability to stress.

In the ambivalence theory view, the impulsivity and separation anxiety of the borderline patient can both presumably be traced to the same defect in ego development that led to the failure to synthesize self and object representations of opposing affective coloration. Thus, impulsivity, to the extent that it appears to have an "oral" quality, would reflect the frustration of very early needs for oral gratification that Kernberg (1966, 1967, 1968) believes to lie at the root of the borderline patient's aggressive feelings toward the primary object; while separation anxiety would reflect the feared loss of the "good" object secondary to the expression of these same hostile aggressive affects.

## OBJECT RELATIONS IN THE NONREGRESSED STATE

Although object constancy is relatively well maintained by the borderline patient in the nonregressed state, he lacks entirely the capacity for mature object love: He is unable to integrate his aggressive feelings toward the object to achieve a balanced and realistic view of him. Relationships with objects are of a need-gratifying nature, such that objects are constantly sought to allay an unconscious but pervasive sense of inner emptiness (Meissner 1982, *DSM-III*). Fear of abandonment, in contrast, is conscious and explicit, contributing to the frustrating circularity of the borderline experience—the same "need-fear dilemma" that Burnham, Gladstone, and Gibson (1969) first described with reference to schizophrenia.

In the ambivalence theory account, both the need-gratifying quality of the borderline patient's relationships and his conscious fear of abandonment would be seen as reflecting the frustration of very early needs for oral gratification as well as subsequent experiences of rejection at the hands of primary objects. The "inner emptiness" of the borderline patient—which I view as the fundamental source of his vulnerability to regression—would be explained in terms of a kind of reactive withdrawal from the intrapsychic representation of the needed but feared object, in anticipation of its loss secondary to the expression of aggression. Meissner's (1982) understanding of the psychopathology of the borderline personality in terms of the paranoid process is an example of this type of explanation.

## SELF-COHESIVENESS IN THE NONREGRESSED STATE

Although the self generally functions in a fairly well-integrated fashion, its cohesiveness is subject to narcissistic vulnerability of the type described by Kohut (1971, 1977), issuing, in the nonregressed state, in such common "fragmentation" experiences as not feeling real, feeling emotionally dull, or lacking in zest and initiative. Further evidence of narcissistic vulnerability lies in the rapidity with which these patients establish what may at first appear to be stable mirror or idealizing transferences in psychotherapy, and their grandiosity or narcissistic idealization of others in everyday life. Ambivalence theory would account for this tenuous cohesiveness of the self in terms of the failure to synthesize contradictory introjective components around which the self is organized (Meissner 1982).

## REGRESSION

Regression brings forth all the more florid psychopathology upon which most descriptions of the borderline personality are based. It can occur gradually, as the therapeutic relationship unfolds, or more precipitously, in response to excessive tension arising within dyadic relationships involving family members or friends. In therapy it is typically preceded by growing dissatisfaction and disappointment with the therapist, particularly with reference to weekends or vacations, and a growing sense of inner emptiness. When it emerges full-blown, it is marked most prominently by clinging and demanding behavior of such intensity as to suggest the patient has lost all capacity for impulse control. Capacity to modulate affects is similarly compromised, with rage reactions of striking intensity following upon the patient's feeling that the therapist is insufficiently available or insufficiently able to satisfy demands. Object constancy is impaired as a result, with the patient unable to draw upon whatever introjects of the therapist he may previously have formed. In the felt absence of these introjects, intense incorporative feelings are mobilized, issuing in wishes to be held, fed, touched, and ultimately merged together. Loss of self-cohesiveness is manifested in hypochondriacal concerns, feelings of depersonalization and loss of integration of body parts, fears of "falling apart," or a subjective sense of losing functional control of the self. Tendencies to devaluation and depression emerge, resulting in feelings of worthlessness and self-hatred. In general, the deeper the regression, the greater the likelihood that primary process thinking will predominate, and the greater the trend for patients to equate impulses and fantasies with fact. There may be transient psychotic episodes, with a generally swift restoration of reality testing (Frosch 1964, 1970).

All of this ambivalence theory of borderline psychopathology would explain in terms of the need to protect the "good" object from aggressive affects arising out of the patient's intense dependency, oral envy, and primitive oral sadism. Specifically, the loss of impulse control would be attributed to ego weakness in the face of powerful oral drives; the onset of rage to equally powerful and equally untamed aggressive drives. The full mobilization of primitive defenses—projection, projective identification, and, most prominently, splitting—would then account for compromises in object constancy. Incorporative feelings would be linked to oral-level drives, loss of self-cohesiveness to the division of introjects around which the self is organized. Finally, primary process thinking would be viewed, again, as reflecting general ego weakness.

## Ambivalence or Insufficiency?

What is noteworthy in the ambivalence theory account of borderline functioning in the realm of object relations is its virtually singular emphasis on issues of orality and aggression as an explanatory basis for psychopathology. This leads, in turn, to a tendency to view certain crucial forms of psychopathology as reactive or secondary to the basic orality/aggression axis, and a concomitant tendency to underestimate the power and influence of these forms in regression. Thus, ambivalence theory views separation anxiety in the nonregressed state as reflecting the feared loss of the "good" object secondary to the expression of hostile aggressive affects, and "inner emptiness" in the nonregressed state in terms of a kind of reactive withdrawal from the intrapsychic representation of the needed but feared object, in anticipation of its loss secondary to the expression of these same affects. Insufficiency, in other words, results from an inability to tolerate ambivalence toward whole objects. In this view, borderline patients form dependent relationships with their therapists because they cannot make adequate use of introjects of persons toward whom they feel ambivalent. When dependency needs inevitably go unsatisfied by the therapist, the patient's frustration issues in aggressive feelings toward him, consequent ambivalence, separation anxiety, and inner emptiness. The whole cycle, that is, is repeated.

My own clinical experience suggests the utility of a different theoretical approach, one that is based primarily on the finding that the regressed borderline patient invariably reports an intensification of his subjective sense of inner emptiness throughout the regression sequence to such a degree that he experiences what I have termed "annihilation panic": He feels not only the lack of wholeness characteristic of the loss of self-cohesiveness, but also—and crucially, in my view—the subjective sense that his self is very near to disintegrating. In this regard, I think it noteworthy that, in significant contrast with my findings, nowhere in the ambivalence theory literature is annihilation viewed as an issue in borderline regression.* To be sure, the subjective sense of threatened annihilation can easily be mistaken for the more objectively observable expressions of disorganizing borderline rage. But I would attribute this omission in ambivalence theory to a more basic problem, having to do with its premises: Annihilation is not an issue for ambivalence theory because, in its account, the self as subjectively perceived is not fundamentally threatened by its incapacity to make use of introjects of persons toward whom it feels ambivalent. That is to say, if the primary issue for borderline patients is the need to keep apart introjects of contrasting affective coloration, then there must already have been substantial solid development of positive introjects around which the self is organized. While ambivalence toward the whole object may then lead to a lack of *self-cohesiveness*, it does not issue in the felt threat of annihilation. Only a theory that views insufficiency as pri-

---

*Little (1981), on the other hand, who uses a different framework, makes annihilation anxiety a focal point of her work.

mary—and not merely a secondary or reactive expression of ambivalence—can fully account for the borderline patient's "annihilation panic" in regression. In other words, only a *primary* inner emptiness, based on a relative *absence* of positive introjects around which the self is organized, can adequately explain the borderline patient's vulnerability to feelings that his very self is at risk.

To my mind, this theoretical focus on a first-order insufficiency of sustaining introjects lends itself to a clearer and more parsimonious explanation of separation anxiety and inner emptiness in the borderline disorder. I would note, in this regard, that the ambivalence theory view has difficulty accounting for inner emptiness in the first instance: According to ambivalence theory, the borderline patient's inner world is, far from empty, relatively *rich* in introjects both of a positive and negative quality. This is not to say that inner emptiness—or, for that matter, separation anxiety—cannot at times intensify in reaction to familiar psychodynamic forces; they can. It is to say, however, that both of these phenomena can only be given their appropriate weight in terms of an explanation that views them as first-order, not second-order, influences on psychopathology.

We can also consider the implications of this position for a psychoanalytic theory of ego functioning in borderline regression. With the ambivalence theory account, I would agree that borderline regression does not substantially threaten the intactness of reality testing, or does so only in transient psychotic episodes, because the self and object representations of the borderline patient remain largely separate, and his use of projection and projective identification is not usually manifested to a degree that significantly obscures his separateness from the therapist. I would further agree that his impulsivity and tendency to primary process thinking can both be attributed to general ego weakness. It

is on the question of the *origin* of this weakness that I depart
from the ambivalence theory account. Thus, while it is
unquestionably true *at a later point in development* that the
ego is weak because it is organized around contradictory
introjective components, and that ambivalence toward the
whole object delays or hinders identification with the functions of positive introjects and subsequent structuralization,
it seems to me, again, both clearer and more parsimonious
to attribute general ego weakness to a *relative absence* of
positive introjects in the first instance, particularly in the
light of the pervasive inner emptiness that I view as the
primary source of borderline psychopathology.

# Two

# Developmental Issues

Developmental findings played a large part in the formulation of the thesis that I have put forward as an explanation for borderline psychopathology. Indeed, the borderline patient's relative or total inability to maintain positive introjects of sustaining figures in his present or past life can always be traced, in my experience, to real loss, relative neglect, or overindulgence alternating with neglect in the patient's history. Accordingly, this chapter is devoted to a discussion of developmental issues and their relevance to the fundamental psychopathology of the borderline disorder.

## Development of the Structural Components of the Inner World

Normal development results in the individual's achieving significant autonomy in maintaining a sense of basic security. In this, two qualities of developmental experience are especially involved. One is narcissistic, having to do with feelings of personal value. The other, more fundamental quality of experience is described by the terms "holding" and "soothing." In infancy the subjective sense of being soothingly held requires the caretaking of a "good-enough mother" (Winnicott 1953, 1960). To some extent, real interpersonal relationships always remain a resource for psychological holding, but with development certain intrapsychic structures play an increasingly prominent role. The advent of object representations provides a means by which resources of holding-soothing can be recognized and, eventually, sought out in the environment. Transitional objects are "created" (Winnicott 1953) in part from intrapsychic components. Later on, the holding function of external objects (and transitional objects [Tolpin 1971]) is internalized in the form of introjects. Finally, identifications with these functions of external objects and introjects yield structural components of the ego that serve the same purpose. In these ways infant, child, adolescent, and adult become increasingly able to provide a subjective sense of security to themselves from their own intrapsychic resources, depending less and less on the environment for it.

## OBJECT REPRESENTATIONS

"Object representations" constitute the substrate for introject formation and the foundation for structural development of the ego. They are conceived here as constructions with purely cognitive and memory components, not in themselves containing affective, libidinal, or aggressive qualities and performing no active functions (Sandler and Rosenblatt 1962, Meissner 1971). Such representations correspond to Sandler's (1960) concept of "schemata": intrapsychic "models" of objects and self (p. 147). He ascribes formation of schemata to the "organizing activity" of the ego (pp. 146–147).

## HOLDING INTROJECTS

I follow Meissner (1971, 1978) in viewing "introjection" as a means of internalizing object relationships, especially as they play a part in gratifying instincts and fulfilling survival needs. Introjects are the internal structures thus created for the purpose of carrying on these functional qualities of external objects in relationship to the self. For the purposes of this study, a simplified view of introjects, likening them to internal presences of external objects, is adopted. Introjects, as such, are experienced as separate from the subjectively sensed self (Schafer 1968), functioning quasi-autonomously in relation to the self, and exercising influence on the self, with the self in a dynamic relationship with them.

Concepts of introjection and introjects are in fact quite complex, especially as they involve projective processes that endow introjects with qualities derived from the self as well as from external objects, and as they relate to internal modifications of the self. Since the focus here is on a particular kind of introject—one that promotes in the self a feeling of being soothingly held—and because, in dealing with the borderline personality, we are concerned with levels of development at a time in infancy when the inherent capacity for self-soothing is very slight and can provide little resource for a projective contribution, we can adopt the more simplified view of introjects as straightforwardly internalized structures that act as resources to the self for holding—"holding introjects." Later on in normal development, and in definitive treatment of the borderline personality, introjective processes, and identificatory processes as well, promote modifications of the self such that it takes on attributes of its holding resources. In this way internal resources are developed for holding, which are more or less integrated with the subjective ego core. These can then serve as contributions via projection to the further formation of holding introjects.


## INCORPORATION AND FUSION

"Incorporation" and "fusion" are modes of internalization developmentally prior to introjection that can have an important influence on structuralization. Incorporation designates the mode by which one person, while in the presence of another, experiences the other person as if "inside" himself, yielding a sense of that person's qualities, for example, warmth or inspired thinking, as if they were merging into his own self. Meissner (1971) writes of incorporation as "the most primitive, least differentiated form of internalization in which the object loses its distinction as object and becomes totally taken into the inner subject world" (p. 287). Operationally, this would be accomplished through volitional suspension of attention to the delimiting contours of the other person's psychological, and perhaps even physical, self. While incorporation can be described as primitive in terms of modes of internalization, in the mature adult it constitutes, along with fusion, a means by which the experience of intimacy—and thereby holding-soothing security—is attained.

Incorporation allows the infant, toddler, or adult to experience an inner suffusion of soothing warmth from the presence of an external holding object. (Of course, prior to differentiation of self from object, this incorporative experience is not under elective control.) When memory capacities develop, these incorporative experiences can be remembered and can have, as Meissner (1971) noted, a structuralizing influence, structuralization conceived here as proceeding from memory schemata organized into merged self and object representations that can then, through introjection of the external object's functional contribution to the incorporative experience, achieve introject status. Further structuralization can occur through identification, by means of which the ego develops a pattern of functioning like that of the introject.

Fusion is the counterpart of incorporation in that the self is felt as merging into the emotional, and perhaps physical, being of the other person. For persons who have achieved differentiation of self from objects, fusion would seem to involve volitional decathexis of ego, and even physical body, boundaries. Like incorporation, it is a means of gaining a sense of intermixing with qualities of someone else. As phenomena of object relating, both incorporation and fusion are important in experiences of intimacy and can occur together.

These comments on incorporation and fusion are particularly relevant in discussion of the borderline personality because of the importance of both in sustaining the self, in influencing the formation of introjects, and, as will soon be discussed, in posing a seeming threat to survival.

## THE INNER WORLD

The concept of the inner world, as elaborated by Hartmann (1939) and Rapaport (1967), is useful in thinking about psychopathology and therapeutic work with borderline personalities. The concept holds much in common with that of the representational world, as described by Sandler and Rosenblatt (1962).

Although ideas about the inner world are very complex, it is viewed more simply here as a kind of psychological internal environment that contains, among other things, self and object representations and introjects. The inner world is not included in the subjective sense of self.

## DEVELOPMENT OF MEMORY, TRANSITIONAL OBJECTS, AND THE INNER WORLD

In my view, memory configurations are basic to the means by which the infant and toddler gain some autonomous capacity for providing themselves with a sense of being soothingly held. Piaget (1937) described six stages in the infant's development of an "object concept," two of which bear particularly on this discussion. Stage IV begins at age 8 months. At this point the infant first gains the capacity to recognize an object as familiar even though he cannot yet evoke the memory of the object without the aid of visual cues.* Fraiberg (1969) terms this capacity "recognition memory." Its development makes possible the begin-

---

*Piaget's stages III to VI trace the development of early memory capacity. In stage III (ages 5 to 8 months), a baby will make no attempt to retrieve a toy hidden behind a pillow even though the toy is placed there while the baby is watching. Apparently, no memory for the object exists. In stage IV (ages 8 to 13 months), the infant will look for a toy that has been hidden behind something while he is watching. He has gained the capacity to remember an object for a few seconds. With stage V (13 to 18 months), the infant will pursue and find a toy that has first been placed behind one pillow, then removed and hidden behind a second; however, the child must *see* the movement from one place to the other. If the second hiding is done by sleight of hand, he makes no effort to search beyond the first hiding place. Not seeing the changes in the object's location, he apparently loses his image of it. Finally, with stage VI (at 18 months), the infant will continue to look for the toy even when the second hiding is done without his seeing it. Piaget concludes that only when the child reaches stage VI does he possess a mental representation of the object as retaining permanent existence despite the fact that it leaves the field of his perception.

nings of an inner world of object representations, one that allows the infant to recognize his mother as familiar and on that basis experience a sense of inner soothing. At the same time not-mother is now recognized as not familiar, resulting in "stranger anxiety" (Fraiberg 1969).

The development of recognition memory coincides chronologically with the beginning use of transitional objects (Winnicott 1953). It is, indeed, a prerequisite for such use—the creation of transitional objects depends upon recognition memory capacity. Because the holding function of the mother is especially effected through the medium of touch, it is hypothesized here that the infant is enabled to maintain ongoing awareness of the recognition memory schema of his soothing-touching mother through actually holding and feeling the touch of a familiar object (the "cue") that reminds the infant of mother's touch. Simultaneously the transitional object serves as an actual resource, by way of the infant's manipulations, of sensory stimulations that, when combined with the sustained memory of the mother, are adequate to induce actual soothing.

Stage VI of object concept development begins at about 18 months of age. At this time the infant gains the capacity to remember an object without being reminded of its existence by external cues. Fraiberg (1969) terms this achievement "evocative memory." According to Sandler and Rosenblatt (1962), the development of the representational world depends on this degree of memory capacity; it might be said that at this time the formation of *continuously available* object representations commences. When the object representation is converted to introject status through internalization (introjection) of the influential functions (attitudes, affects, and impulses) of the person after whom the object representation is patterned, the former purely cognitive memory schema takes on a functional capacity: As an introject, it can perform for the self certain functions, such as holding, that previously were performed by external objects; at the same time, it takes on the affective qualities of the object associated with those functions. The development of evocative memory capacity is thus a prerequisite for introject formation and subsequent structuralization of the ego.

The holding introject derived from the relationship with the soothing mother enables the toddler to manage for a while out of the sight of and at some distance from his mother without suffering separation anxiety (Mahler, Pine, and Bergman 1975). Over time, holding introjects are progressively stabilized; to some extent they remain important resources throughout life against depression or anxiety that could result from separations.

The acquisition of enduring holding introjects also puts the toddler or child in a position to give up the tangible transitional object. According to Winnicott (1953), the transitional object then becomes to some extent diffused into certain areas of experience with the external world, especially the area of culture. Experience with the transitional object can also be internalized in the form of an introject or an identification—according to Tolpin (1971), by means of "transmuting internalization."

## Fundamental Psychopathology of the Borderline Personality

The fundamental psychopathology of the borderline personality is in the nature of developmental failure: *Adult borderline patients have not achieved solid evocative memory in the area of object relations and are prone to regress in this area to recognition memory or earlier stages when faced with certain stresses.* The result is relative failure to develop internal resources for holding-soothing security adequate to meet the needs of adult life. To repeat, the formation of holding introjects—of both past and present figures—is quantitatively inadequate, and those that have formed are unstable, being subject to regressive loss of function. As might be expected, object representations of sources of holding are also vulnerable to regressive loss. The developmental failure appears to result from mothering that is not good-enough during the phases of separation-individuation (Mahler, Pine, and Bergman 1975). Although the toddler is ready for the neuropsychological development of memory needed to form representations and introjects, the environment does not facilitate it.

## GOOD-ENOUGH MOTHERING AND DEVELOPMENT OF MEMORY

In this regard, Bell's (1970) important study suggests that those children who seem to have had the most positive maternal experience developed the concept of person permanence—for example, "mother permanence"—before the concept of object permanence—for example, "toy permanence"—and achieved earlier mastery of the stages of permanence for both persons and objects than did children whose mothers were rejecting. These latter children, in contrast, tended to develop object permanence before person permanence, and were delayed when compared to the former group in achieving the highest stage of permanence for both objects and persons. Let us consider the reasons why this should be so.

Achievement of the capacity for evocative memory is a major milestone for the 18-month-old child and a most significant step in his developing capacity for autonomy. No longer does he depend so fully upon the actual presence of mother for comfort and support. Instead, he has acquired some capacity to soothe and comfort himself with memories and eventually introjects of his mother and of his interactions with her. But this is a *developing* capacity: It is fragile in the 18-month-old child and readily lost at least transiently if he is stressed by too long a period of separation.

Robertson and Robertson describe, in their film (1969) and commentary (1971), a 17-month-old boy, John, who was left in a residential nursery for nine days while his mother was having a baby. John had had a good, healthy relationship with his mother. Although the staff of the nursery to which John was entrusted cared about children, no one staff member took responsibility for any one particular child. Moreover, the staff came and went, with changing shifts and days off. When John, with his background of good individual mothering, attempted repeatedly to reach out to various staff members for the consistent individual care he needed, he was unable to obtain it, in large part because the other children there—chronically institutionalized—had become expert in aggressively seeking out whatever attention there was to be had. Over the nine days of his stay, John changed from a friendly child to one who cried and struggled to return home when his father visited. Later he grew sad and forlorn, then angry; finally he withdrew into apathy, ate little, and could not be reached by anyone who tried to comfort him. He took solace, often desperately, and with inadequate results, in a large teddy bear.

I would argue that, at 17 months, John was well on his way to achievement of evocative memory capacity. With the loss of his mother, however, he suffered a regression from this nearly achieved capacity to an earlier level of development: recognition memory and nearly exclusive reliance on a transitional object—the teddy bear, with which he tried to evoke the experience of being soothed. I shall return to the case of John in Chapter 3, giving further evidence in support of my view. For now it is enough to examine the relationship it suggests between consistent mothering and the development of memory.

For the infant with only recognition memory capacity, the presence of the transitional object is necessary in order to activate and maintain an affectively charged memory of the soothing mother; he is unable to evoke an image of his mother without the aid of visual or tactile cues. At the same time, of course, the use of transitional objects represents a significant step forward in the development of autonomy: The infant can soothe himself in the mother's absence for longer and longer periods by using the transitional object to evoke memories of her holding-soothing qualities. Use of the transitional object thus represents a "prestage," as it were, of the capacity to *abstract* the mother's qualities from her actual person. But it is *only* a prestage, in the sense that these qualities must still be embodied in an object temporally connected with the mother's recent presence. When this temporal connection becomes sufficiently attenuated—when the mother is not available often enough—the relationship between her qualities and the qualities of the transitional object is itself attenuated, and the child can no longer make effective use of it to soothe himself. Conversely, when this relationship is reinforced by the mother's consistent availability, the embodiment of her qualities in the transitional object is solidified. Although her qualities do not yet have abstract existence in the mind of the infant, they are more and more abstracted *from* her.

Even before the development of neuropsychological capacity for evocative memory, then, the infant is "primed" by his experience with the transitional object for the eventually full abstraction of his mother from her person that is the hallmark of evocative memory. Neuropsychological maturation and the use of transitional objects thus go hand in hand in the development of solid evocative memory. When both have developed to a sufficient degree, the child can begin to evoke the memory of mother without the aid of external cues. But the capacity for evocative memory is itself only imperfectly achieved at this stage. The good-enough mother must still be available often enough to provide actual holding and soothing security to whatever extent evocative memory remains insufficient for that purpose. In the mother's too-prolonged absence, the child is liable to seek consolation in the transitional object. But since the effective use of the transitional object depends, as we have seen, on the mother's consistent availability, *and* since its effective use is a prerequisite for the development of evocative memory, the mother's too-prolonged absence leads to a breakdown in whatever capacity for evocative memory has already been achieved. The *foundation* of evocative memory in the use of transitional objects is compromised, as evidenced by the child's inability to achieve holding-soothing security from the object itself. John's case is an example: His use of the teddy bear did not, finally, console him.

There is no better evidence for the initial instability of evocative memory, and the contribution of good-enough mothering to its eventual stabilization, than that afforded by Mahler's description of the rapprochement subphase (Mahler, Pine, and Bergman 1975). At about 15 months of age, she points out, or three months before the achievement of solid evocative memory, the child becomes particularly sensitive to the absence of mother. Whereas previously he could explore the environment with confidence and vigor, returning to mother only for food, comfort, or emotional "refueling," he now becomes increasingly concerned about her exact whereabouts. His subsequent behavior alternates between stout independence and clinging. Apparently, the development of upright locomotion, which allows the child to travel some distance from the mother, when combined with the beginning development of evocative memory, brings clearly to the toddler's attention the fact of his psychological separateness from her. But since the capacity for evocative memory is not yet sufficiently established to provide holding-soothing security in the mother's absence, she must still be available for that purpose. Her presence, in turn, facilitates the further development of memory capacity. In the absence of good-enough mothering, in contrast—whether because of unavoidable traumatic separation, inconsistency of supportive presence, aversive anger, or purposeful abandonment—solid evocative memory capacity does not develop. To whatever extent it *has* been achieved, it constitutes an inadequate basis for the formation of object representations, holding introjects, and subsequent structuralization, and remains vulnerable, throughout life, to regression in the face of stress.

## ANNIHILATION ANXIETY

In my clinical work, I have generally been able to document one or a series of traumatic events in the second or third year of life that has led to the borderline patient's failure to develop solid evocative memory. In my view, the borderline patient's pervasive fear of abandonment by significant figures in his adult life can usually be traced, in a dynamic as well as a genetic sense, to this failure (although failures at other stages of separation-individuation can compound his vulnerability). To put the matter as briefly as possible, since holding introjects of present and past figures are functionally inadequate by virtue of the instability of the memory basis for their formation, the borderline patient lacks the capacity to allay separation anxiety through intrapsychic resources. In other words, in the absence of such resources, separation threatens the loss of holding-soothing security. In order to appreciate more fully what separation means for the borderline patient—what is at stake for him—let us first consider his experience at the very earliest stage of infant development.

At about 4 weeks of age, Mahler (1968) states, most infants break out of the condition of "normal autism" into which they are born. For the next three to four months the newborn's survival and continued well-being depend on a condition of "symbiosis" with the mother. By such a condition Mahler refers to "that state of undifferentiation, of fusion with mother, in which the 'I' is not yet differentiated from the 'not I,' and in which inside and outside are only gradually coming to be sensed as different" (1968, p. 9). The mother, in this connection, functions as the infant's "auxiliary ego" (Spitz 1965). Her ministrations augment the infant's rudimentary faculties through what Mahler terms "the emotional rapport of the mother's nursing care, a kind of social symbiosis" (1968, p. 9). From a functional standpoint, the symbiotic bond replaces the infant's inborn stimulus barrier; it becomes the functional means of protecting the infant from stress and trauma. Infant and mother, in the mind of the infant, constitute "an omnipotent symbiotic dual unity" (Mahler, Furer, and Settlage 1959, p. 822), and the infant tends to project all unpleasurable perceptions —both internal and external—outside the protective symbiotic "membrane."

In this very earliest stage of development, then, the infant's sense of well-being cannot properly be spoken of as "subjective." It is only gradually—within the secure confines of the symbiotic relationship, and in the course of need gratification by the mother—that the infant comes to recognize an external reality—a "not I"—that extends beyond his self-boundaries and that is at first represented by the mother. Even then, he is unable fully to experience himself as differentiated from the mother; the mother necessarily remains a "part object" throughout the symbiotic phase (Mahler, Pine, and Bergman 1975, p. 49). In a crucial sense, then, the mother who is the first *object* of the infant's subjectivity remains an essential *aspect* of that subjectivity—is unified with it. Subjectivity is thus at risk in two senses when the child is separated from the mother: Not only is the object of subjectivity absent—the "not-I"—but also the dual unity that *is* the infant's psychological existence—the "I," to whatever extent we can speak of an "I" in this very early, relatively undifferentiated state.

Subjectivity in its earliest form is *intrinsically* connected with the mother's holding-soothing presence; it cannot exist without it. Thus can we understand what is at stake for the child who has not developed evocative memory capacity or who has lost it in consequence of regression: In the absence of any capacity to bring before the mind what is not actually present, the child's separation from mother threatens his very subjectivity—his sense of subjective being. That is to say, the mother's absence feels to him like a threat to his psychological *existence*, because, in its earliest form, that existence is intrinsically connected to the mother's holding-soothing presence.

This formulation allows me to account for two important aspects of my thesis. First, it explains the prominence of annihilation anxiety in borderline *regression*: For the borderline personality, the basic cause of anxiety is the threat of the loss of the self through psychological disintegration as a consequence of being abandoned. In regression, with the serious threat or condition of abandonment—

with the therapist's being insufficiently available, for example—the borderline personality's separation anxiety intensifies beyond the signal level and is experienced as a threat to his psychological self—a threat of annihilation. It remains only a threat, however. The serious compromises in subjectivity that are the outstanding feature of psychosis are rarely seen, and then only transiently, because borderline patients have generally had sufficient experiences of holding-soothing to develop a basic sense of subjective being—of psychological separateness, which eventuates in psychological selfhood. Although this sense of subjective being is less solid than ambivalence theory would have us believe—in that it is subject to the felt threat of annihilation—it is *more* solid than that of the psychotic—it only rarely breaks down *in fact*. Thus, whereas the regressed psychotic patient experiences the *collapse* of subjectivity (the fusion of self and object representations), the regressed borderline patient experiences the felt *threat* of its collapse. Indeed, the fact that the threat *is* subjectively experienced suggests the basic intactness of subjectivity in the borderline patient. My formulation, then, accounts for the differences between psychotic and borderline regression, and at the same time clarifies the comparability of the issues at stake in each— their identical *basis* in the area of subjectivity.

I am also prepared now to address an objection that might be raised against my larger thesis: If evocative memory capacity in the borderline patient is inadequate for the formation of sufficient, and sufficiently stable, holding introjects, then how can it be adequate to the formation of *hostile* representations and introjects, which are relatively *abundant* in the borderline personality's inner world? In this regard, I would note, first, that the inadequacy of holding introjects is relative. Evocative memory capacity has developed to sufficient extent to permit the formation of *some* holding introjects, however unstable and subject to loss they might be in the face of regression. The problem then becomes one of accounting for the relatively greater number of hostile introjects. And in this regard, I would refer the reader to the corollary of Mahler's conception of an "omnipotent symbiotic dual unity": that the infant tends to project all unpleasurable perceptions, both internal and external, outside the protective symbiotic membrane. The reason for the disparity, then, is that the infant's reactive hostility is a plentiful resource via projection for formation of negative representations and introjects. But since the infant possesses little *innate* resource for holding-soothing, and must rely on good-enough mothering for it, there is less experience available for formation of positive representations and introjects when mothering is inadequate.

# Three

# Psychodynamics of Borderline Psychopathology

In elaborating my thesis, I am all too aware that I have had to anticipate to some extent the evidence on which it is based. In this chapter I shall present this evidence in some detail, in terms of the characteristic psychodynamics of the borderline patient in treatment.

## Holding Selfobjects

Because their internal resources for holding-soothing are always inadequate, borderline personalities depend in an ongoing way upon external objects to supplement them enough to keep their muted anxiety at a signal level and to maintain relative psychological stability. I use the term "selfobject," which was first defined in relation to the use of objects by narcissistic personalities (Kohut 1971, 1977;

Gedo and Goldberg 1973), to designate the various persons used for this purpose. The essence of the selfobject is that it provides functions for another person that are necessary to maintenance of psychological integrity but that cannot be adequately performed by the other person for himself. The selfobject is so designated because it is experienced as part of the self.

For the narcissistic personality, the selfobject is needed to maintain a sense of self-worth by providing a mirroring function or by serving as an object of idealization. Failure of the selfobject function threatens not only serious depression but also loss of cohesiveness of the self. For the borderline personality, the selfobject is mainly required to provide forms of holding-soothing, without which he is faced with the ultimate threat of disintegrative annihilation of the self. In my experience borderline patients invariably use their therapists as "holding selfobjects." Their clinging and demanding behavior can be viewed as characteristic of a failure of this use.

## Rage and Regressive Loss of the Sustaining Inner World

By virtue of relatively good adaptation to reality and relatively good object relating, the borderline personality by and large maintains sufficient interaction with holding selfobjects to avoid intense separation anxiety. Crises occur, however, when excessive tension arises in the dyadic situation with regard to the friend's or therapist's insufficient availability in the face of the patient's escalating demands. In either case the impetus for regression is the failure of friend or psychotherapist to perform the holding function to the degree needed. This is experienced by the patient as a threat to his "entitlement to survive," and there is no more assured way to induce the characteristic rage of the border-line patient than this. Indeed, under such circumstances, borderline rage can be annihilatory in intent and intensity. In the words of one patient, she "'stomps'" the therapist out of her mind. The result of this annihilatory rage is the compounding of the perceived external threat of abandon-ment with a greater or lesser degree of loss of internal resources for holding. This comes about in two ways.

One is purely psychodynamic and quite common. The patient feels the impulse to reject and destroy the offending therapist. In the regressed state he is more under the sway of primary process thinking, so that he tends to equate impulses and fantasies with fact. The patient feels as though he has evicted the felt image of the good therapist (the holding introject) from his subjective inner world. More-over, the urge to destroy the therapist is felt as an accom-plished act; this primitive mode of thinking about the ex-ternal object is then reflected in his inner world, where the corresponding introject also seems lost.

The other way in which intense rage diminishes in-ternal resources for holding is more important and is par-ticular to borderline personality psychopathology: Rage induces a loss of functional use of holding introjects, repre-sentations, and transitional objects by virtue of a regression of cognitive quality that specifically affects the memory foundations of these resources. In terms of the infant, anni-hilatory rage brings about greater psychological separation from the mother than is conducive to the stability of evoca-tive memory capacity, in accordance with our earlier understanding of the connection between the mother's availability and the development of that capacity. Indeed, since rage is precipitated by inadequate mothering in the first place, it may be viewed as exacerbating the infant's sense of having been abandoned. Similarly, rage felt toward the therapist or friend induces, by virtue of the same process, regressive loss of evocative memory and subsequent loss of introjects, representations, and transitional objects.

The sequence of the regressive loss is the reverse of that of the development of these psychological entities. Thus the regression can extend through two levels. The first level I have called "recognition memory rage," because with enough separation anxiety and consequent rage there is loss of evocative memory for the holding selfobject. In fact, regressed borderline patients commonly report an inability to remember the affective image of the therapist's face or voice outside therapy hours. Loss of evocative memory is then reflected in functional loss of both the holding introject and the sustaining object representation based on the selfobject. In this sector of the inner world, in other words, there seems quite literally to be a regression to Piaget's stage IV of object-concept formation, with only recognition memory available: Rage is directed at the selfobject that is recognized as depriving. Still, use of the external holding selfobject remains possible through direct interpersonal contact, and transitional objects remain useful as resources for holding-soothing, depending as they do on at least a level of recognition memory for their functioning. If, however, separation anxiety and consequent rage intensify even more, a second stage of regression is precipitated in which the use of recognition memory is also lost. The external object is then no longer recognizable as a potential source of holding, and resort to transitional objects is no longer possible. Some patients report an inability to recognize the therapist even while in his presence. This situation is termed "diffuse primitive rage," characterized as it is by the unchanneled, generalized discharge of hate and aggression. At this point separation anxiety becomes annihilation panic.

John's case provides an example of recognition memory rage. The reader will recall that John was separated from his mother for nine days. On the ninth day his parents came to take him home. Robertson and Robertson (1971) described his reaction as follows:

> At the sight of his mother John was galvanized into action. He threw himself about crying loudly, and after stealing a glance at his mother, looked away from her. Several times he looked, then turned away over the nurse's shoulder with loud cries and a distraught expression. After a few minutes the mother took him on her knee, but John continued to struggle and scream, arching his back away from his mother and eventually got down and ran crying desperately to the observer. She calmed him down, gave him a drink, and passed him back to his mother. He lay cuddled into her, clutching his cuddly blanket but not looking at her.
>
> A few minutes later the father entered the room and John struggled away from the mother into the father's arms. His crying stopped, and for the first time he looked at his mother directly. It was a long hard look. His mother said, "He has never looked at me like that before" (p. 293).

As I have already suggested, it appears that John regressed from a nearly achieved capacity for evocative memory to an earlier level of development: recognition memory and nearly exclusive reliance on a transitional object. His inability to be comforted and the look he finally gave his mother can be understood as representing recognition memory rage. When John recognized his mother, the rage he had earlier manifested, before regression to stage IV, came bursting forth: He gave her a "long hard look," then resolutely turned away from her and clutched his blanket. This recognition memory rage also seems to include active avoidance of her and an identification with the aggressor. The same kind of rage, with detachment and tantrums, continued through the first weeks after he returned home. In the Robertsons' paper, John is contrasted with other children of his age who were placed in foster homes where the needs of the child were well understood and met; for them such regressive behavior was minimal.

## Loss of Cohesiveness of the Self

Although the borderline personality is subject to feeling vulnerable to annihilatory disintegration, his sense of self is sufficiently developed to avoid it. In my experience, however, the borderline personality is subject to more severe manifestations of loss of *self-cohesiveness* than Kohut (1971) describes for narcissistic personalities. *Cohesiveness of the self in borderline personalities is as dependent on an equilibrium of holding-soothing as it is on self-worth,* so that failures of holding in their relations with external objects can precipitate not only separation anxiety but also loss of such cohesiveness. In this sense, loss of self-cohesiveness may be viewed as the penultimate stage of a process that ends with the felt threat of self-disintegration (whereas self-disintegration is not at issue for narcissistic personalities). I have observed manifestations of this loss of cohesiveness especially as degrees of incoherency or disjointedness of thinking, as feelings of loss of integration of body parts, as a subjective sense of losing functional control of the self, and as concerns about "falling apart." Disruption of self-cohesiveness in itself causes anxiety, but never of the intensity of annihilation panic.

# Incorporation, Fusion, and the Need–Fear Dilemma

As discussed in Chapter 2, incorporation and fusion are modes of intimacy by which a person can experience a feeling (for example, soothing) as if through psychologically intermingling with a related quality (for example, holding) of another person. Because of his relative dearth of holding introjects, the borderline personality must seek such intimacy with holding selfobjects. When he is under the influence of intensified separation anxiety and regressively deprived of the use of holding introjects, the impetus toward incorporation and fusion is urgent and mandatory. At the same time, however, these modes of gaining soothing are also felt as representing a threat of destruction of the self and/or the selfobject, and the greater the need, the greater the felt threat becomes. When the borderline personality is in relatively good equilibrium, this threat is well controlled by adjusting interpersonal closeness: not so close as to be too threatening, not so distant as to leave the patient alone. Sometimes the equilibrium is maintained by diffusing the sources among many selfobjects, not allowing prolonged intimacy with any one of them. Or it may be possible to maintain a steady regulation of the degree of closeness with one or a few relationships. Finally, relating may be characterized by rather rapid oscillations between several relationships, each of which is experienced intensely for a brief time.

One patient provides an example of this process. To the therapist she complained that the "boys" she met were uncommitted to her, i.e., unwilling to satisfy her needs. As she became able to separate her demands and projections from the real qualities of these men, it became apparent that they were passive, inhibited, obsessional people who were frightened of involvement with women, especially involvement with a woman as demanding as she. When gradually she became able to control the intensity of her demands, she became involved in a relationship with a warm man who fell in love with her and pursued her for herself, specifically for the healthy aspects of her personality. Her response was one of terror, a sense of being smothered, and a conviction that the man was weak, helpless, and ineffectual (as she often described herself). She also felt a murderous rage, with wishes to tear at him and strangle him. Thus, her attempt to accept a genuinely warm relationship evoked her fears of fusion, a transient breakdown of self boundaries, and a massive use of projective identification. It readily became understandable why she had chosen uncommitted and distant men to begin with.

One threat that both incorporation and fusion seem to pose arises out of the quality inherent in these experiences that involves loss of attention to the separate and defined existence of the self or other. Under the influence of intense need, the awareness of the defined existence of self or selfobject is sacrificed in the interest of maintaining the need-satisfying experience, but the price is bearing increasing anxiety about the destructive dissolution of the self or selfobject that seems to be inherent in these modes of relating. In this sense, then, incorporation and fusion implicate both sides of the subjectivity coin: Incorporation threatens the "not-I," fusion the "I." And this even though each mode comes into use precisely because experiences of holding-soothing have been inadequate in the first place to the solid development of the subjective sense of the self. Thus the borderline dilemma: Too little closeness threatens the psychological self, too much the very same thing. And yet the latter tends to follow inexorably from the former.

A greater threat resides for the borderline personality in the fact that incorporation and fusion also involve oral-level impulses, and the more intense the need for holding-soothing, the more intensely are oral impulses mobilized. It is the impulse to eat or absorb the selfobject concomitant with psychological incorporation that, in the fantasy representation of it, involves literal destructive consumption of the selfobject. Similarly, the wish to be eaten or absorbed by the selfobject concomitant with psychological fusion involves fantasy representation of literal destruction of the self. The more intense the need, the more intense are the impulses, wishes, and fantasies. The more regressed the patient, the more primary process dominates, to the point that the borderline personality can experience vivid fears because he believes that what must be done to avoid annihilation anxiety will only involve him in destroying the selfobject upon which he depends for survival, or in being destroyed himself. With progress in psychotherapy these fears gradually emerge into consciousness. The patient must also deal with horror in finding cannibalistic impulses within himself, especially as they are directed at people whom he loves. Although this need-fear dilemma is overtly evident only in a regressive state, especially as it occurs in the progressive course of treatment, *at an unconscious level* it pervades all relationships of a holding-soothing nature.

It is here that one finds the reason that the borderline personality has not been able to correct the developmental defect central to his psychopathology, even though he may have been involved in many trustworthy, caring relationships subsequent to early childhood. These fears, predominantly at the instinctual, but also at the object-relational, level, prevent the steady, trusting holding-soothing relationship over time that constitutes the necessary facilitating environment for the solid development of the subjective sense of self. It is for this reason that incorporation and fusion do not contribute to structuralization in the borderline personality.

## Aloneness: The Subjective Experience Associated with the Primary Sector of Borderline Psychopathology

To the extent that he lacks sufficient holding introjects, the borderline patient is subject to a core experiential state of intensely painful "aloneness," a term that I prefer to "inner emptiness" for allowing us more clearly to distinguish it from the related affective states of "loneliness" and "sadness." In my terminology, loneliness is a state of yearning, often mixed with sadness. Like sadness, loneliness always carries with it the felt sense of the presence of the person or milieu longed for. In theoretical terms, a functional holding introject is a prerequisite for loneliness, and for sadness as well. The pain arises from the real object not being available, and one must make do with the felt presence within while concomitantly wishing for the company of the real object. In contrast, aloneness is the experience that accompanies the need for a real holding selfobject under circumstances of not having an adequately functioning holding introject. It is the experience of aloneness that is central to the borderline personality's subjective being. At its most intense, it is felt as stark panic that threatens annihilation of the self, and with it the issue of separation is absolutely clear. When holding introjects are to some degree functional and some use can be made of holding selfobjects, the feeling of aloneness is diminished. Repression also plays a role in muting it. Still, the unconscious feeling is there in some degree. It may be in the form that Chessick (1974) describes, a feeling of not being really alive, a sort of deadness that he terms, after Federn, a "defective ego-feeling." In his observations the role of separateness, of the need for holding contact, is very clear. Masterson (1976) describes another form of what may be termed "attenuated aloneness," a "sense of void," which is a feeling of "terrifying inner emptiness or numbness." The sense of void is often felt as pervading the environment too, so that one is surrounded by meaninglessness and emptiness.

These affective experiences could all be subsumed under depression, but it is a special quality of depression related to relative inadequacy of holding. One witnesses it in extreme form only in crises or regressed states. So far as can be determined, these lesser degrees of it are not elsewhere in the literature ascribed to an actual developmental deficit of resources for holding. Instead of there being an absence of intrapsychic structure, the general view is that the problem lies in the presence of introjective structures that exert a negative influence. I have already cited Meissner's (1982) understanding of the psychopathology of the borderline personality in terms of the paranoid process as an example. Masterson (1976) expresses views along the same lines, yet comes closer to my position. He ascribes the sense of void in part to "introjection of the mother's negative attitudes that leaves the patient devoid, or empty, of positive supportive introjects" (p. 42). Modern literature deals with the subject of aloneness abundantly but always, it seems, in these attenuated forms, usually in terms of defenses and desperate ways of coping with it. Chessick (1974) notes this element in *The Stranger* by Albert Camus. Other examples are Virginia Woolf's *The Waves*, Joyce Carol Oates's *Wonder-*

*land*, and Thomas Pynchon's *The Crying of Lot 49*. Many patients also refer to Eduard Munch's painting *The Scream* as a depiction of their emotional state of aloneness.

Borderline patients are, of course, to the extent they have use of holding introjects, capable of sadness. But the sadness that depends upon tenuously functional introjects is hard, in that it lacks tenderness, and is desperate in quality, often frightening to the patient because he feels the edge of terror in it and fears that he will fall into it. Two patients described a photograph that conveyed this particular form of intense, fearful sadness. It was a famous one that appeared in *Life* magazine at the time of the Japanese attack on China. It shows a lone infant sitting with eyes closed, crying, screaming, amid the rubble of a Shanghai railroad station a few seconds after its mother had been killed by a bomb. Another patient, for whom the experience of aloneness seemed like a primary given, traced it as far back as a memory from infancy. Her mother had in fact been unable most of the time to be with her. The patient recalled lying in a crib pervaded by a desperate sense of isolation; she did not, however, call out, because she knew no one would come. What is noteworthy in this case is that the patient's report of this memory included no remembered imago of her mother and no remembered hope that her mother would come to her, suggesting the early breakdown of evocative memory.

In "The Capacity to Be Alone," Winnicott (1958) wrote in theoretical and experiential terms that are altogether compatible with the concepts being advanced here. Because of my debt to Winnicott, and because of confusion that might otherwise arise, I wish to clarify that what I call aloneness Winnicott referred to as not being able to be alone or not being able to enjoy solitude. The person whom I would say is capable of being comfortable by himself, without the presence of others, Winnicott referred to as a person capable of being alone by virtue of the presence of a "good object in the psychic reality of the individual" (p. 32). I would say that such a person is subject to loneliness rather than aloneness.

# PART TWO
# Psychotherapy of the Borderline Patient

# Four

# Treatment of the Primary Sector of Borderline Psychopathology

Definitive treatment of the primary sector of borderline psychopathology involves three successive phases. In this chapter I shall outline the work involved in each, and illustrate it with aspects of a clinical case. Because the narcissistic sector can bear in a particular way on the primary sector, it is also noted.

## Phase I: Inadequate and Unstable Holding Introjects

The primary aim of treatment in the first phase is to establish and maintain a dyadic therapeutic relationship in which the therapist can be steadily used over time by the patient as a holding selfobject. Once established, this situation makes it possible for the patient not only to develop insight into the nature and basis of his aloneness but also to acquire a solid evocative memory of the therapist as sustaining holder, which in turn serves as a substrate out of which can be formed adequate holding introjects. That is, developmental processes that were at one time arrested are now set in motion to correct the original failure. This process would simply require a period of time for its occurrence were it not for certain psychodynamic obstacles that block it in therapy just as they block it in life. These obstacles must, therefore, receive intensive therapeutic attention. They are consequences, or corollaries, of aloneness. The inevitability of rage is one such corollary that interferes with the process of forming holding introjects. This rage has three sources for the borderline patient:

1. Holding is never enough to meet the felt need to assuage aloneness, and the enraged patient is inclined to vengeful destruction of the offending therapist, of a fantasied eviction of the therapist from the patient's psychic inner world. Under these circumstances the patient feels as if he imminently will, or even has, lost or killed the therapist. In addition, the patient expects to lose the therapist through the therapist's responding to his rage by turning from "good" to "bad" in reaction to the patient's hostile assault and rejection.

2. The holding selfobject that does not meet the need is not only the target for direct rage but is also distorted by means of projection of hostile introjects. Thus the patient carries out what he experiences as an exchange of destructiveness in a mutually hostile relationship; subjectively, the inevitable re-

sult of this projection is the loss of the good holding object.

3. The object that is so endowed with holding sustenance as to be a resource for it is deeply envied by the needy borderline patient. This envy necessarily involves hateful destructive impulses.

Any of these sources of rage can lead to the state of recognition memory rage or diffuse primitive rage, with transient loss of holding introjects or object representations or even loss of use of transitional objects. At such times the patient is subject to the terrifying belief that the therapist has ceased to exist. When that occurs all possible support of the holding-soothing type may be required to maintain his psychic integrity and stability.

There is another corollary to aloneness that acts as a serious impediment to the process of forming a holding introject. It is the intensity with which the borderline personality must employ incorporation and fusion as a means of experiencing holding with a selfobject, an intensity that involves oral impulses as well as experiences of psychological merging. Belief in the imminence of destruction of the selfobject, the self, or both, demands that the borderline patient distance himself from his selfobject to such an extent that the subjective experience of holding-soothing is not adequate to promote the needed development of solid holding introjects.

There is yet one more impediment to the use of the therapist as a holding selfobject. It is a primitive, guilt-related experience that involves the belief by the patient that he is undeserving of the therapist's help because of his evilness. The patient's response is akin to the negative therapeutic reaction (Freud 1923) in that it can lead to the patient's rejection of all therapeutic efforts, as well as his rejection of the real relationship with the therapist, in the service of self-punishment. In extreme situations it can lead to suicide attempts. Primitive guilt can generally be traced to an archaic punitive superego.

Acquiring insight into and working through the impeding corollaries of aloneness—threats posed by rage from various sources, incorporation and fusion, and primitive guilt—are necessary in order for the borderline patient to be in a position to use his selfobject relationship with the therapist over time to develop a stable evocative memory for and introject of the therapist as holding sustainer. Treatment in phase I, therefore, focuses on these dynamic impediments to the use of the selfobject therapist for attaining the desired intrapsychic development for experiencing stable holding-soothing. Each of these impediments must be worked with in the standard ways as it manifests in transference, through use of the therapeutic maneuvers of clarification, confrontation (see Chapters 7 and 8), and interpretation. Once insight is gained, each aspect requires working through. This treatment must be conducted in an adequately supportive therapeutic setting, one that attempts insofar as possible to help maintain the tenuous holding introjects and internal objects, hence keeping annihilation anxiety within tolerable levels and maintaining cohesiveness of the self. The amount of support may considerably exceed that involved in most psychotherapies. To some extent the therapist in reality acts as a holding selfobject. Transitional objects (for example, vacation addresses and postcards), extra appointments, and telephone calls reaffirming that the therapist exists are required at various times, and, for the more severely borderline personalities, one or two brief hospitalizations may well be expected. At times, in the interpersonal setting of the therapy hour, the therapist must vigorously clarify, interpret, and confront the patient with reality, especially around matters of the therapist's continued existence as a caring object, his not resembling the hostile introjects or identifications that the patient projects, and the patient's minimization of dangerous situations in which he may, through acting out, place himself when struggling with these issues. When splitting of the type Kernberg (1967) describes occurs acutely with the danger of serious acting out, it requires priority attention for correction.

The outcome of this work with the impeding corollaries of aloneness is this: The patient learns that the therapist is an enduring and reliable holding selfobject, that the therapist is indestructible as a "good object" (Winnicott 1969), that holding closeness gained by incorporation and fusion poses no dangers, and that the patient himself is not evil.

Indeed, the initial increments in development of a holding introject take place as the patient begins to believe in the survivability of the therapist as a good object. Hope is aroused that the relationship and the therapeutic work, involving understanding of object and selfobject transferences plus genetic reconstructions, will open the way for psychological development and relief. Once the holding introject gains some stability, a positive cycle is induced that results in a diminution of the intensity of aloneness and, along with it, a diminution of the corollary impediments; this in turn allows for further development and stabilization of holding introjects.

The healing of longstanding splitting (of the type Kernberg [1967] describes)—in the relationship with mother, for example—must await this formation of stable holding introjects. *Efforts to bring together the positive and negative sides of the split can be therapeutic only after development of more stable holding introjects along with correction of distorting projections that have acted to intensify the negative side of the split.* Development or recognition of realistically based love on the positive side of the split is also helpful in healing it. With these therapeutic developments, the external and internal resources for love and holding become sufficient to endure the acknowledgment that the loved and hated object are one and the same and that the loving and hating in one's self toward the object must be reconciled.


## CLINICAL ILLUSTRATION

Mr. A. began treatment in his mid-twenties when, as a graduate student, his lifelong sense of depressive emptiness grew dramatically more intense and he was progressively enveloped by diffuse anxiety, issuing in suicidal feelings. He had been very successful in his field of study and was highly regarded by his professors and peers, but he had no truly close friends. Those who did gain some intimacy with him found themselves repeatedly rebuffed as he time and again withdrew on some pretext into an irritated reserve, often then drawing closer to someone else. The person who most often occupied his mind was his mother, usually with a sense of rage. He respected his father as a hardworking, semiskilled man with principles. In his own pursuits as a student he was rather like him, but his father was a reserved man who was dominated by his wife and related to the patient mostly at a distance. His mother was often emotionally involved with the patient, but always in terms of her own wishes and needs and rarely, if ever, in terms of him as a separate person with his own identity. Alternately she was either intensively close or preoccupied with herself to such an extent that she appeared to have forgotten him. She involved him in sensuous body closeness, only to repel him in disgust when he responded. When angry she would declare that she had made him and she could kill him, and as a child he believed it. She also had clinical episodes of depression, during which she would take to bed and become literally unresponsive to everyone. Nevertheless, she was a compelling person for the patient. She was beautiful, and the positive times of closeness with her were heavenly. She gloried in his high intelligence and always backed his efforts to achieve academically.

From early childhood, at least from age 3, he was repeatedly sent by his mother to live with her childless sister for periods of weeks, up to a year. At times her motivation seems to have been the need to ease her burdens while having a new baby. The aunt and uncle were kindly and quiet but did not relate well to the boy. He felt desolate, describing these visits away from his mother as like being stranded on a frozen desert. Sometimes he could manage his feelings with blissful fantasies of being harmoniously close to his wonderful mother, but he could not sustain them.

As twice-a-week psychotherapy deepened over a period of months, the patient felt increasingly dependent on the therapist. Looking forward to seeing him began evolving into an urgent sense of missing and needing him between hours. Longing was mixed with anxiety; by the time a year had passed, he began to express anger that the therapist was not with him enough and did not care enough. The transference evolved into a clear projection of his introjected relationship with his mother, which was clarified and interpreted. Insight was of little value, however, as he began to experience times with the therapist as wonderfully helpful and times away from him as a desert-like isolation where, despite continued good academic performance, all other involvements most of the time seemed meaningless.

As rage with the therapist intensified, the patient stopped looking at him. For the next two years, he never looked directly at the therapist, finally explaining that he was so full of hate toward him that he felt that his gaze would fragment the therapist's head into slivers of glass.

His intense yearning for the presence of the therapist contrasted with his increasing aloofness in the hours. The distancing behavior extended further. On entering and leaving the office, the patient began walking along a path that was as far away from the therapist as the room contours and the size of the doorway would allow. Whenever the therapist moved forward a little in his chair, the patient with a look of fear moved as far back in his chair as he could. Clarification of his apparent fear of closeness led first to emergence of overt fear that on entering and leaving the office he might fall into the chest of the therapist and disappear; similarly, he feared the therapist's leaning forward in his chair because it felt like the therapist could fall into the patient's chest and be totally absorbed. None of these fears were at the level of delusion, but the fantasy was so intense that it dictated behavior. Tentative interpretations of the possibility that his fears involved a wish led to emergence of overt cannibalistic impulses, first discovered in a dream that involved eating meat, which he recognized as the therapist, and later emerging in a dream of the therapist as a large-billed bird who was going to eat the patient.

As rage with the therapist mounted, the patient began acting out in consciously self-destructive ways. He started drinking straight whiskey in bars noted for homosexual perversion and violence, thinking about the therapist and saying to himself, "I'll take what I have coming!" It was in this part of therapy that he experienced nearly intolerable times when he could not summon any memory image of the therapist beyond a vague inner picture. He could not sense the feeling of being with the therapist; he described these times as very frightening periods of belief that the therapist did not exist. On one such occasion he drank heavily and in a rage of aloneness and annihilation panic recklessly crashed his car into the side of a bridge. The therapist responded with added vigor in interpreting the patient's transient incapacities to know that the therapist existed. He insisted that at such times the patient must not act on his fear and rage but must instead telephone the therapist and, if necessary, make extra appointments. The therapist emphasized that in this way the patient would have a chance to learn that the therapist did continually exist, did continually remember the patient, and really was available to him. The patient did as the therapist urged, contacting him with brief calls and occasionally seeing him extra times as a means of managing these crises. (For a more detailed account of this episode, including a fuller analysis of Mr. A.'s homosexual feelings, see Chapter 7.)

In these ways the therapist was attempting to help the patient bear and understand his aloneness, rage, regressive memory loss, and frightening belief that closeness meant mutual destruction through incorporation and fusion. The clear transference to the therapist as a seductive and abandoning mother led to genetic interpretations and insight. But it also was essential that the patient repetitively have the opportunity to learn that despite his rageful attacks on the therapist, the therapist remained a caring person who consistently tried to help. For example, the patient spent 40 minutes of one hour verbally assaulting the therapist. He hated him intensely and wanted to kill him. He was certain the therapist did not understand what he was going through, that he couldn't understand how he felt because he did not care—he only collected the fee. He absolutely wanted to kill the therapist, to crash into him, drive his car into his house and smash it, rip it apart as though it were canvas. He hated the patient who preceded him and thought that she was in analysis, getting a higher form of caring than he was. He wanted to run over people in the neighborhood with his car and run over the therapist. He knew the therapist's family was there in the house, and he wanted to kill them too. He expressed all this with great intensity, feeling at the time that he really meant it. But with the therapist's persistent attitude of attentive acceptance, the patient in the last 10 minutes grew calmer, saying finally that his problem really was that he wanted to possess his therapist completely, literally to swallow him whole.

With all of these efforts the patient gained a steady capacity to remember the therapist and to feel what contact with him was like at times between hours. He stopped having to make emergency telephone calls. His rage diminished. He began looking at the therapist, and he developed comfort with his wishes for incorporative and fusion closeness.

He told about a fantasy that he had had since childhood and now attached to the therapist. He was quite fond of it. It first developed after he learned about slaughterhouses for cattle. What he yearned for was closeness with the therapist gained through their each having been split down the abdomen so that their intestines could mingle warmly together. It was clear from the way he told it that this was a loving fantasy.

## Phase II: The Idealized Holding Therapist and Introjects

In general the holding introjects established in phase I are considerably unrealistic, in that they are patterned in part after qualities of whatever positive introjects were formed in early years. As such they are idealized in a childlike manner. The selfobject transference is strongly colored by projection of these idealized introjects, and introjection of this transference experience results in formation of an idealized holding introject that the patient takes to be a homologue of the holding qualities of the therapist. Were treatment to stop here, the situation would be quite unstable, for two reasons. First, the unrealistic idealization of the holding introjects, along with the projections of them onto persons who serve as holding selfobjects, would continually be confronted by reality and would inevitably break down. Second, at this point the patient is still heavily dependent on a continuing relationship with holding selfobjects (including the therapist), as well as holding introjects, for an ongoing sense of security; this is not a viable setup for adult life, in which selfobjects cannot realistically be consistently available and must over the years be lost in considerable number.

The therapeutic work in phase II parallels that described by Kohut (1971) in treating the idealizing aspects of selfobject transferences with narcissistic personalities. (Indeed, the introjects of interest here are idealized not simply in the area of holding, but also in terms of worth. For purposes of this discussion, the two qualities that are idealized are artificially separated, and the one concerned with worth is addressed in a later section.) Kohut describes the therapeutic process as "optimal disillusionment," and the term is applied in this section to idealization in the area of holding-soothing as he uses it in the area of self-worth. No direct interventions are required. The realities of the therapist's interactions with the patient and the basic reality orientation of the patient always lead to the patient's noticing discrepancies between the idealized holding introject, based on the therapist and reflected in the transference, and the actual holding qualities of the therapist. Each episode of awareness of discrepancy occasions disappointment, sadness, and anger. If each disappointment is not too great, that is, is optimal, a series of episodes will ensue in which insight is developed and unrealistic idealization is worked through and relinquished. (Any disappointments that are greater than optimal precipitate recurrence of aloneness and rage in a transient regression that resembles phase I.) Ultimately the therapist as holding selfobject is accepted as he realistically is: an interested, caring person who in the context of a professional relationship does all that he appropriately can to help the patient resolve conflicts and achieve mature capacities. Holding introjects come to be modified accordingly.

## CLINICAL ILLUSTRATION

At this point, Mr. A. was preoccupied with interrelated idealized holding introjects based on good childhood times with his mother and unrealistic beliefs about the therapist. Directly and indirectly he declared strongly positive feelings for his therapist. He was not concerned about vacations, because he knew the therapist kept him very much in his thoughts. He fantasied their hugging in greeting when the therapist returned (something that he in fact never attempted). At the same time he reminisced tearfully about the passive bliss of being with his mother at the times she cared for him. He referred to her by her first name, Joanna.

He grieved repeatedly as he recognized, little by little, that the idealized images of Joanna and the therapist were unrealistic. This work required no active stimulus from the therapist; reality intruded on idealizing illusion enough to keep the work going. The therapist helped the patient bear his grief and put it into perspective by empathically staying with him, by providing clarifications and interpretations about dynamic and genetic bases for his disappointments, and by avoiding any confrontations that would intensify his disappointments. The grief process consisted of sadness, crying, nonmurderous anger, and relinquishment of impossible yearnings.

For example, for several weeks the patient had talked tearfully about how beautiful life had been with Joanna. She was everything to him, and he would do anything for her. He also spoke of the solidity he felt in his relationship with the therapist. It was like the large oak trees that stood outside his office. Then in one hour he related a dream in which he was descending the stairs of an elevated streetcar station. There were several people on the ground waiting for him, including a woman and the therapist. He noticed that the stairs ended several feet above the sidewalk and he was expected to jump. The people could have made it easier by catching him, but it was safe enough; so they simply stood by watching. He was angry, jumped anyhow, and was all right. After reporting the dream he said that he had been wishing the therapist would talk to him more. He didn't know much about the therapist personally and really longed to know more. He felt deprived, and he was angry about it. He felt jealous of other patients and the therapist's family; they all got something special from the therapist. He wanted to be like a man in a recent movie who lived to be adored. He wanted all his therapist's adoration. He wanted him to smile affectionately, touch him, clean him all over, touch and clean every crevice of his body, like a mother would her baby. He was jealous of people whom he fantasied the therapist to be close to sexually. The wonderful thing the therapist had to give was like two golden pears in his chest. He yearned for them so much and did not get them. He was furious about it, felt like destroying them. Then he became sad, and tears streamed down his cheeks. He felt badly about his anger because he knew that what he wanted was unreasonable. The therapist said to him that it was like his dream. He wanted to be held in his jump to the sidewalk although he knew he actually didn't need it. His anger arose not because a need to be saved was ignored, but because he wasn't receiving something he very much yearned for. Mr. A. agreed that this was the meaning of his dream and was the way he felt.

The excerpt that follows is taken from the last portion of Phase II. The patient said:

> I feel like I'm missing Joanna, like I'm looking for her everywhere, and she ought to be all around, but she's not. [He looked mildly depressed and sad.] I miss her. I miss her, and you can't bring her back, and nobody can. It's like she died. [He began to laugh.] I wonder what the real Joanna is like. The Joanna I yearn for isn't the real one at all. It's some ideal Joanna I'm wanting, someone very wonderful and very exciting. A Joanna like that never really existed. [He grew sad, but retained his humor.] You know, the trouble is that I don't see people and places for what they really are because I keep looking for Joanna there. There are lots of girls I know but haven't ever appreciated because I haven't really related to them. I've missed out on them. I had a dream. All I remember is that there was a wonderful celebration for me, but I couldn't enjoy it because Joanna wasn't there. It's like part of me has died, but it's not so much that I can't do okay without it. It's really as if she's been everywhere or is everywhere. She's part of me, and it's awfully hard to give her up. [With good humor, slightly hypomanic.] It feels like I can peel Joanna off now, that it's like a layer of skin. And when I do, most of me is still left there very solid.

# Treatment of the Narcissistic Sector of Borderline Personality Psychopathology

The majority of borderline personalities also exhibit serious pathologies of narcissism of the type Kohut (1971, 1977) and Goldberg (1978) describe, manifested in everyday life by grandiosity and narcissistic idealization of others and in psychotherapy by apparently stable selfobject transferences of the mirroring and idealizing types. I shall be discussing the relationship between narcissistic and borderline psycho-pathology in greater detail in Chapter 5. For now it is enough to note that by and large the modes of treatment delineated by Kohut are applicable to treatment of the narcissistic sector, but that the therapeutic work is compli-cated by the interrelationships of pathological narcissism and pathology of holding-soothing the self. There are three concerns here:

1. Narcissistic grandiosity and idealization can substi-tute for holding-soothing in effecting a subjective sense of security. Some borderline personalities make significant use of this substitution as a regular part of their character functioning; others tem-porarily resort to it as a means for feeling secure at times when use of holding selfobjects is compro-mised. Perhaps this substitution is effected through the medium of the satisfaction and pleasure inherent in possessing or partaking of perfection, as well as through the assurance and security offered by the sense of invulnerability that accompanies narcissis-tic grandiosity and idealization.
2. Cohesiveness of the self depends upon maintaining

equilibrium in the areas both of narcissism (Kohut 1971) and of holding-soothing.

3. Although dynamically different, undermining of pathologically maintained narcissism can be a life-and-death matter, as can the loss of the borderline personality's means of maintaining holding-soothing of the self. Undermining of grandiosity or idealization can precipitate a subjective experience of worthlessness that is unbearably painful. By itself it does not, as aloneness does, portend danger of annihilation, but it can prompt serious suicidal impulses as a means of gaining relief and/or punishing whoever is felt to be responsible (Maltsberger and Buie 1980).

The importance of pathological narcissism for maintaining a subjective sense of security and self-cohesiveness and for avoiding unbearable worthlessness bears greatly on the timing of therapeutic approaches to narcissism in the borderline personality. Insofar as possible, pathologically maintained narcissism must not be weakened during phase I of treatment, when holding-soothing security is so vulnerable and the risk of aloneness, with annihilation anxiety and loss of self-cohesiveness, is so high. In phase II, narcissistic idealization and grandiosity are often interwoven with idealizations of the holding type. At this time therapeutic disillusionment can often be successful in both areas, provided it remains optimal for both. It may be necessary, however, to delay definitive treatment efforts with the narcissistic sector until after the work of phase II is accomplished in the primary sector of borderline personality psychopathology. Timing must, of course, vary from patient to patient. The guideline is that narcissistic issues can be approached only insofar as a stable holding selfobject transference and adequately functioning holding introjects are firmly enough established to prevent regression into insecurity and loss of self-cohesiveness.

For Mr. A. narcissistic pathology was not extreme. It was expressed in phase II especially in the context of the idealized holding selfobject transference—in feeling and wanting to feel adored. Optimal disillusionment in the area of holding proceeded hand in hand with optimal disillusionment in the area of narcissism.

## CLINICAL ILLUSTRATIONS

Ms. B., a 25-year-old social worker, by documented history had since infancy suffered intermittent rejections by her immature and volatile mother, as well as excessive verbal and physical abuse. She exhibited in her history and in therapy a narcissistic developmental arrest of the type Kohut describes, along with the elements of a borderline personality. She was especially fixated at the level of a grandiose self through having been very important to her mother as an idealized selfobject. For her mother's sake and her own she needed to be outstandingly bright and popular. In late grade school the equilibrium between them began to disintegrate under the impact of her real position vis à vis her peers and teachers. The intense urgency and importance of her needs had made her a socially awkward girl, and the tension lest she fail to achieve perfection had immobilized her in academic competition. As her position with teachers and peers deteriorated, she tried to meet her mother's and her own needs by lying to her mother, conveying fantasies of achievements and popularity as if they were facts. Eventually her gullible mother learned the truth, and the narcissistic equilibrium of each was permanently shattered.

Treatment in phase I was more difficult with Ms. B.

than with Mr. A. In addition to problems with aloneness, she was subject to desperate feelings of worthlessness when her selfobject means of maintaining narcissistic equilibrium were threatened or interfered with. This added extra dimensions of intensity to the therapy, including greater levels of rage and envy, and at times the therapist had to provide vigorous support to her fragile sense of self-worth. In phase II she worked through her idealizations of the therapist as selfobject holder and modified her introjects accordingly. Thereafter some effective work was done with her pathological narcissism; in phase III it became possible to modify her need for grandiosity by substituting self-worth derived from effective involvement in personally meaningful pursuits and achievements. Although at termination narcissistic pathology still persisted significantly, follow-up has shown that the process that began in treatment continued. Successful life experiences made possible further replacement of the grandiose self and idealizing transferences with realistically rewarding career achievements and more realistic involvements with worthwhile people.

Certain patients who are insecure because of relative paucity of holding introjects and relative inability to use holding selfobjects may exhibit considerable pathological narcissism yet require little direct therapeutic work with it. These are patients who use pathological means of maintaining narcissism as a substitute form of security that supplements their inadequately available means of maintaining holding security. A third case illustrates this pattern.

Mr. C. was a successful historian whose background included marked deprivation of security from the time of infancy. He was a brilliant man, however, and he possessed outstanding charm of a mannered sort. He was preoccupied with this image of himself and loved to indulge in fantasies of being Henry VIII and other magnificent men of history, often in affairs with great women of the past. But all his relationships were emotionally shallow, and his mannered charm obscured the fact that he had no close relationships, including with his wife and children. They often entered into playing out his fantasies of being a king whom they obediently revered. The magnetism of his personality was such that a great many people quite willingly provided the mirroring admiration that he needed to maintain his fantasy life.

Mr. C. was able to live well financially by virtue of an inheritance; this was a most important prop for his grandiosity. When the money ran out, he decompensated into a prolonged phase of severe depressions alternating with mania, at times exhibiting evidence of delusions. On several occasions he attempted suicide. Finally, he began psychotherapy with the aim that it be definitive. He desperately reached for closeness with the therapist, probably for the first time in his adult life, and soon was involved in the therapeutic situation that has been described for phase I. Concomitantly he reconstituted his old grandiosity, using the therapist as a transference mirroring selfobject. As with Ms. B., this part of the psychopathology was not worked with and was not challenged in phase I. When he entered phase II, he was in a well-established selfobject transference of the holding idealization type. Unlike Ms. B., however, he now altogether discontinued his transference use of the therapist, or other people, to support his pathological narcissism. At the same time more realistic modes of maintaining self-worth emerged. Prior to his decompensation he managed the primary sector of his borderline psychopathology by maintaining a guarded distance in all relationships and by supplementing the inadequate resources for holding in his inner and external worlds with substitute security derived from maintaining a grandiose self. Once an adequate stable idealizing transference of the holding type was established in phase II, he was able to and did essentially dispense with his grandiose self (apparently permanently) because he no longer needed it for security.

## Phase III: Superego Maturation and Formation of Sustaining Identifications

To become optimally autonomous—that is, self-sufficient—in regard to secure holding and a sense of worth requires two developments: (1) A superego (as an agency comprising both the conscience and the ego ideal) must be established that is not inappropriately harsh and that readily serves as a source of a realistically deserved sense of worth. (2) The ego must develop the capacity for pleasurable confidence in the self (the heir to grandiosity) and for directing love toward itself that is of the affectionate nature of object love.* This development of the capacity to love the self in the manner of object love contributes not only to enjoyment of being one's self but also makes possible a reaction of genuine sadness in the face of losses that involve the self—accident, disease, aging, approaching death—a grief that is homologous with that experienced with object loss. Without

---

*Object love is differentiated from narcissistic love in that object love is attached to qualities of the object that do not necessarily serve purposes for oneself and are not vicariously felt as if one's own; the reward of investing with object love is simply the experience of affectionately loving the other person. Narcissistic love centers around qualities of worth and survival that involve qualities of oneself, or qualities or functions of another person that are felt as enhancing personal value and survival. Although love feelings may be associated, narcissistic love is rewarding only insofar as self-experiences of worth and security are somehow enhanced.

this ego development, the reaction is instead one of depression, fear, and despondency, which typify "narcissistic" loss rather than object loss.

The therapeutic endeavors in phase III are based on the principle that capacities to know, esteem, and love oneself can be developed only when there is adequate experience of being known, esteemed, and loved by significant others.

Once the inappropriately harsh elements of the superego (or superego forerunners) have been therapeutically modified, the process by which superego development is initiated in this phase of treatment is introjection, as described by Sandler (1960). Accordingly, early in this sequence of development, one can speak of superego forerunners that have the quality of introjects in the psychological inner world, that is, of being active presences that exert an influence on the ego. For example, a patient might state, "I can feel how my therapist would guide me and value me for this work." Such superego-forerunner introjects evolve into an agency, one that still functions with the quality of an introject; through a process of depersonification, however, it comes to be experienced as part of the self rather than as part of the inner world. One can now speak of a superego and illustrate this development by altering the example just given into, "My conscience guides me and gives me approval for pursuing this work well." Further development occurs through increasing depersonification and proximity of the superego to the "ego core" (Loewald 1962), along with integration of the superego with the ego. These developments can properly be subsumed in the concept of the process of identification (Meissner 1972), and it is in this way that superego functions are ultimately assumed as ego functions. Now the ego is no longer in the position of being responsive to the influence exerted by an agency external to it but, rather, becomes its own guardian of standards of behavior and its own source of a sense of worth. At this point the example under consideration evolves into, "I feel good about this work of mine which is in line with my values and meets my standards."

Often these patients also require help to gain the capacity to experience subjectively the factualness (validity) of their esteemable qualities, as well as the capacity to experience feelings of self-esteem. This process requires the transient selfobject functioning on the part of the therapist that will be described in the clinical section that follows.

In this phase of treatment, the ego evolves as its own resource for pride and holding through development of intrasystemic resources that are experienced as one part providing to another, both parts being felt as the self. These ego functions are developed through identification with the homologous functioning of the therapist as a selfobject. That is, the therapist, verbally at times, but largely non-verbally, actually does provide the patient with a holding function, a function of loving in the affectionate mode of object love, a function of validating (enhancing the reality valence of) the patient's competences, and a function of enjoying the exercise and fruits of the patient's competences. To varying degrees these functions are internalized, first in the form of introjects, but in phase III they become depersonified and increasingly integrated with the ego, ultimately becoming functions of the ego by means of identification. This is the process that Kohut (1971) designates as transmuting internalization. The experiential quality of these newly gained ego functions might be expressed as follows: (1) "I sustain myself with a sense of holding-soothing"; (2) "I love myself in the same way that I love others, that is, affectionately, for the qualities inherent in me"; (3) "I trust my competence in managing and using my psychological self and in perceiving and interrelating with the external world; hence I feel secure in my own hands"; and (4) "I enjoy knowing that I am competent and exercising my competence."

The impetus toward effecting the introjections and identifications involved in these superego and ego developments arises out of a relinquishment of the therapist as an idealized holding selfobject, as well as a relinquishment of whatever use has been made of him as a narcissistic transference selfobject. Such relinquishment also involves homologous modification of introjects in the inner world that have been patterned after the selfobject transferences. Then the patient is forced by his needs to develop other resources for maintenance of holding security and narcissistic equilibrium. The introjections and identifications just described provide the necessary means for accomplishing this task. They also establish a stability of self in terms of holding and worth that is far greater than was possible before. The depersonified introjections and identifications are by their nature more stable and less subject to regressive loss under stress than the configurations and arrangements they replace (Loewald 1962).

Total self-sufficiency is, of course, impossible. For its healthy functioning the ego requires interaction with the other agencies of the mind as well as with the external world (Rapaport 1957), and no one totally relinquishes use of others as selfobject resources for holding and self-worth, nor does anyone relinquish using selected parts of the environment (art, music, and so forth) as transitional objects (Winnicott 1953). These dependencies are the guarantees of much of the ongoing richness of life.

It is only through the developmental acquisitions of phase III of treatment that the former borderline personality acquires genuine psychological stability. Of course, the degree to which it is achieved varies from patient to patient.

## CLINICAL ILLUSTRATION

Although superego development cannot be divorced from ego development (Hartmann and Loewenstein, 1962), for purposes of clarity a partial and artificial division of the clinical material will be made along this line.

### SUPEREGO DEVELOPMENT

In a time when nearly all hostile introjects had been altered and tamed in Mr. A., it became noticeable that one remained of a superego-like quality. It was like a harsh taskmaster that in fact overly dominated the conduct of Mr. A.'s work life. His associations included one of the dicta belonging to this introject: "You must sweep the corners of the room first; then you will be sure to clean the center." In fact his thoughts had been intrusively dominated by that maxim while cleaning his apartment the day before, and he hated the driven way he worked in response to it. It derived from his mother, being one with which she often regaled him. Further exploration revealed that nearly the entirety of the harsh taskmaster introject phenomenon under study was derived from interactions with this harsh quality of his mother. Although the genesis and present-day inappropriateness of this part of his inner world were clear to the patient, no modifications occurred. In a later hour the therapist, on a hunch, asked whether the patient would miss this harsh-mother-like conscience if it were gone. The question stimulated a mild grief reaction as the patient associatively discovered that he would in fact miss the felt presence of her that was the concomitant of the harshness. Indeed, it became clear that this introject partook of both negative and positive qualities of the interaction with his mother, and it seems for that reason it was the last significantly negative introject to go.

Thereafter a more mature superego began to develop. Mr. A. already possessed appropriate guiding standards as well as the internal authority to promote them (Sandler 1960). Therefore, some of the therapeutic work described above was not required. What he did need was a sense of satisfying and pleasurable self-value. Attaining it was a two-step process. To a degree he "knew" about many aspects of himself that were worthy of esteem, but he did not know them solidly and effectively so that his knowledge could carry the full value, or valence, of reality. The full reality of his positive qualities had, therefore, to be established first. This took place in the therapy through the process of "validation," by which it is meant that the therapist reacted, verbally and nonverbally, to accounts of episodes in which esteemable qualities played a part in such a way as to convey simply that these qualities had registered in his mind as realities. Communication of this to the patient enabled him, then, to experience these qualities with a sense of realness himself. Validation is a selfobject function performed in this way by the therapist; the interaction provides an experience such that the patient can not only feel the realness of his qualities but also gain, through identification, the capacity to validate his qualities himself. The qualities thus covered in therapy by Mr. A. were myriad. His capacities as, by then, a college teacher of sociology constituted one such area. He was very successful with his students and with other faculty members. There were numerous events that demonstrated their appropriate esteem for him, but he was not in a position to understand and appreciate their expressions of esteem or to develop a similar sense of esteem for himself until he related it to the therapist. He could then gain a sense of the validity of their judgment.

The second step in acquiring a capacity for appreciating

his own self-worth was facilitated by another aspect of the therapist's behavior when the patient related such episodes. The therapist responded with appropriate, subtle, but similar expressions of esteem. This directly promoted the patient's feeling an approving esteem for himself. Ultimately, through processes of introjection and identification, he developed a much improved capacity for autonomous self-esteem. He then no longer required it as a selfobject function from the therapist.

EGO DEVELOPMENT

The patient required ego development that involved all the functions referred to in the brief theoretical considerations for phase III of treatment: (1) self-holding, (2) self-love with "object love," (3) trust and security in one's competence, and (4) prideful enjoyment in one's competence. Examples can be given of each.

*Self-Holding.* Originally the patient worried fearfully about his health—signs of illness, being overweight, working too hard, and so forth. But there also was a real basis for his concerns. The therapist never responded with a similar worry, but he did show interest and a warm concern that carried with it the implied message that the patient should care for and take care of himself. Eventually this became the patient's attitude, displacing the old fretful, nonproductive worrying. He began to care for himself with a sensible attitude toward himself; at that time the therapist stopped responding with a selfobject level of involvement. The patient then went on a diet, losing the weight he needed to lose, and he ordered his life better, for example, getting more nearly the amount of rest and relaxation he needed. All in all, it could be said that he developed an essentially autonomous caring about himself that effected a self-holding function.

*Self-Love with "Object Love."* In phase III especially, the patient related many stories of his work and personal life: how he managed a difficult committee problem, how he helped a student advisee who was in serious difficulty, or the conversational interchange with an old friend. Increasingly the full quality of his subjective experience in these episodes was regularly expressed in a spontaneous manner. The therapist in fact liked the patient very much, though he never said so. But his mostly nonverbal listening to these stories certainly conveyed his affectionate enjoyment of the companionship involved in his empathic vicarious participation. Eventually a new attitude emerged in the patient toward himself, one that was implied rather than explicitly stated. It was an affectionate attitude toward himself, one that partook of the quality of affection he felt for other people: his friends, students, and therapist. It was a self-love that mostly differed in quality from the holding form of caring about himself described above—it did not specifically involve concern for himself or taking care of himself, even though it could be combined with these. The therapist surmised that his own love for the patient had been important in the patient's coming to love himself, probably through the mechanism of identification. A further benefit of this development was that in loving himself the patient could more readily acknowledge and accept the love others expressed for him.

*Trust and Security in One's Competence.* Prior to phase III of treatment, the patient was always beset by doubts about his competence to do the task at hand, even though he nearly constantly was called upon, for example, to teach, give speeches, and organize meetings. He was never sure that he could express himself effectively, despite the fact that he never failed to do so. This doubt concerning his competence was present from the beginning of therapy and persisted unchanged for a long period. The therapist's function of validating seems again to have provided the necessary experience to bring about change. The therapist developed a realistically founded judgment that the patient was indeed solidly competent in a large number of ways, and by his attitude conveyed this judgment repeatedly to the patient, although he rarely put it into words directly. Gradually the patient came to regard his competences as facts about himself; they had been validated by the therapist. It seems that the patient finally assumed the function of validation of his competence himself, probably through identification with the therapist's similar functioning. With this development his confidence in himself as he conducted day-to-day matters grew more solid; with it he seemed to gain a significant increment in his overall sense of security. It is as though he now could say to himself with authority, "I can handle what life brings me."

*Prideful Enjoyment in One's Competence.*  The therapist enjoyed the patient's competence, and this, too, was subtly conveyed. As it was with establishing value through superego functioning, so it was with taking pleasure or pride in the exercise of his competence. First he had to know securely that it was "real," valid; then he was in a position to enjoy it. This capacity, too, developed over time in phase III.

## Psychotherapy or Psychoanalysis for the Borderline Personality

The ideas presented here apply mainly to treatment in the setting of two- to five-times-a-week psychotherapy. Some analysts report successfully using the psychoanalytic situation for treating patients broadly described as borderline.

Chase and Hire (1966), for example, employ analytic techniques along with some parameters, and Boyer and Giovacchini (1967) restrict technique to classical procedures.

I believe that very important elements of the treatment are analytical: the development of stable transferences, the use of spontaneous free association along with clarification and interpretation for gaining access to unconscious content, and working through in the context of transference and the living of everyday life. But treatment of the primary sector of borderline psychopathology also requires actual selfobject functioning by the therapist in addition to facilitation of the use and resolution of selfobject transference. In phase I, when the patient transiently loses the capacity to conduct his life safely, the therapist must set limits and otherwise participate in protecting the patient. As regression deepens, there is a need for the therapist to confront the patient with the fact of the therapist's existence and availability, as well as to extend his availability outside treatment hours in order to provide additional actual psychological selfobject holding. Providing transitional objects may at times be necessary, the effectiveness of which may depend on the actual functioning of the therapist as a holding selfobject. In phase III various kinds of subtle selfobject functions are necessary to provide the experience out of which the patient can through introjection and identification gain certain autonomous capacities: to guide and approve of himself according to his ideals, to experience the validity (realness) of his personal qualities, including his competences, to provide himself with a sense of security, and to love himself affectionately. All of these crucial selfobject functions of the therapist fall outside the realm of classical psychoanalysis. More important, these selfobject functions in large measure are effected nonverbally, especially through facial expression and body gesture. As such, the face-to-face context of psychotherapy is facilitating, and for some aspects of treatment essential. For this reason I advocate psychotherapy for phase I of treatment of all borderline personalities. The psychoanalytic format can often be instituted sometime thereafter, depending on psychological qualities of the patient, the therapist-analyst, and their interaction. For borderline patients of higher-level integration, whose holding introjects are more nearly stable, psychoanalysis might be used throughout treatment. In some cases it could even be the treatment of choice.

## Aloneness, Rage, and Evocative Memory

Because of their importance for my thesis, I should now like to restate my clinical findings in terms of three key concepts: aloneness, rage, and evocative memory. Aloneness usually begins to become manifest gradually in the transference as the patient finds the therapist to be a good sustainer or soother. The therapist need not make direct efforts in this regard, for the patient senses that the reliable capacity to sustain is an inherent part of the therapist's personality. The patient relinquishes some of the defensive distancing which he has maintained in various ways to some extent in all relationships. Because he needs to, and sometimes because he has a tenuous trust that it is worth the risk, the patient allows himself to depend on the therapist for sustenance of the holding-soothing variety. As he does so, the extent of his felt need—which corresponds to the extent of his vulnerability to feeling abandoned—comes forcefully to his attention. To varying degrees this need feels overwhelming and uncontrollable as his dissatisfaction emerges that the therapist cannot gratify the intensifying longings that occur in treatment. Usually this feeling begins as an aimless, joyless sense of something missing from his life in the intervals between therapy sessions. Ultimately it develops into episodes of aloneness, preceded and accompanied by a rage that may not be conscious and therefore not verbalizable, felt within himself and in the surrounding environment. And when this experience is intense and accompanied by conscious or unconscious rage, it brings annihilation panic.

I have found that this escalating experience almost always centers around being away from the therapist; it reaches such proportions in an uncontrollable way because the patient finds himself unable to remember the soothing affective experience of being with the therapist, especially as his anger increases. Sometimes he cannot even remember what the therapist looks like. He behaves as if he has largely lost evocative memory capacity in this sector of his life.

The therapeutic task is to provide the patient with an interpersonal experience over time that will allow him to develop a solid evocative memory for the soothing, sustaining relationship with the therapist. Clarification, interpretation, and sometimes confrontation are necessary in order for the patient to gain understanding of his frightening experience and make intelligent use of the therapist's help. Most crucial is the provision by the therapist of adequate support to keep the experience of aloneness within tolerable bounds as the underlying issues, including the patient's rage, are examined. Brief telephone calls to augment a faltering evocative memory are often necessary. At times a patient may need to phone several times a day simply to reestablish on a feeling level that the caring therapist in fact exists. When evocative memory fails more completely, extra appointments are necessary. If the failure is extensive, a period of hospitalization with continuance of therapy hours is crucial.

Clinically the therapist must constantly assess the patient's capacity to tolerate his rage so as to prevent regression to recognition memory or an even earlier stage.

Activity by the therapist that defines the issues, clarifies the meanings and precipitants of the rage, and puts it into terms the patient can discuss also demonstrates the therapist's availability, caring, concern, and reality as a person who has not been destroyed by the patient (Winnicott 1969). The therapist's repeated empathic assessment of the issues around the patient's rage, while simultaneously demonstrating his own survival and existence, supports the patient's faltering evocative and recognition memory capacities. Here, too, hospitalization may be required when the therapist's activities in this area are insufficient to stem the sometimes overwhelming regression into desperate aloneness.

There is yet another way available to the therapist for helping the borderline patient maintain contact with an affective memory of him during absences. It is one that seems specifically indicated in developmental terms, namely, the provision of a transitional object, which is so important to the infant during the time between his recognition of separation from mother and his acquiring the use of evocative memory as a way of maintaining a sense of her soothing presence. Transitional objects specific to the therapist can be useful at these desperate times: the therapist's phone number on a piece of paper or the monthly bill (which the patient may carry in his wallet for weeks at a time). During vacations, a card with the therapist's holiday address and phone number usually are not used in order actually to contact the therapist but, rather, are carried as activators of memories of the absent therapist, just as the blanket is used as an activator for remembering the feel of mother by the infant who has as yet acquired only recognition memory. Fleming (1975) described how, in retrospect, she became aware that asking a patient to monitor his thoughts while he was anxious over weekend separations was a way of helping him evoke her image. I know of several patients who have spontaneously kept journals about their therapy. Through communicating with their journals they activated the feelings associated with being with the therapist.

Whereas Mr. A. could always recognize the therapist once he heard his voice or saw him, that is, he could regain his affective recognition memory of, and sense of support from, the therapist, some borderline patients regress to the point that even when they are with the therapist they are unable to feel, that is, to "recognize," his supportive presence—despite that fact that they can identify the therapist as a person. I have also noted that when treating a colleague's borderline patient during the colleague's vacation, my primary, often sole task is to help the patient retain evocative memory of the absent therapist through talking about details of the patient's experience with him.

The recognition memory–evocative memory framework can be a useful way of defining issues in the process of change in psychotherapy. It can be utilized to monitor a major task in psychotherapeutic work: the goal of helping the more primitive patient achieve a solid use of evocative memory that is relatively resistant to regression. Once the capacity for affective evocative memory for important relationships is firmly established, the patient may be considered to have reached the narcissistic personality to neurotic spectrum.

## Summary

In Chapters 1 through 4 we have seen that the primary sector of borderline pathology involves a relative developmental failure in formation of introjects that provide to the self a function of holding-soothing security. This developmental failure is traced to inadequacies of mothering experience during separation-individuation. Holding introjects

are not only functionally insufficient but also subject to
regressive loss by virtue of the instability of the memory
basis for their formation. Because they are functionally
inadequate to meet adult needs for psychological security,
the borderline personality is constantly subject to degrees of
separation anxiety, felt as aloneness, and is forced to rely on
external holding selfobjects for enough sense of holding-
soothing to keep separation anxiety relatively in check—to
avoid annihilation panic. Incorporation and fusion are the
psychological means of gaining a sense of holding security
from selfobjects. Because of the intensity and primitive
level of his pathological needs, the borderline personality
unconsciously believes that incorporation and fusion also
carry with them the threat of destruction of selfobject and
self. This belief, along with vicissitudes of rage arising out
of unmet need, makes it impossible for the borderline personality to maintain the kind of steady closeness with holding selfobjects in adult life that is necessary for developing a
solid memory base for formation of adequately functioning
holding introjects.

Psychotherapy for his primary sector of psychopathology proceeds in three phases. Phase I involves regression,
with emergence of marked separation anxiety and rage,
transient regressive loss of function of holding introjects
and transitional objects, and emergence into consciousness
of impulses and fears associated with incorporation and
fusion. Clarification and interpretation, limit setting, actual
provision of selfobject holding at a psychological level, and
proof of indestructibility as a good object are the means by
which the therapist enables the patient to understand and
work through the impediments to the use of him as a
holding selfobject. This accomplishment frees the patient to
develop holding introjects based on experience with the
therapist along with other past and present experiences

with holding selfobjects. These introjects are, however, unrealistically idealized in terms of holding. Phase II is concerned with modification of this idealization through a series of optimal disillusionments with the therapist as holder-soother in the context of a selfobject transference. Relinquishing the idealization compels the patient to develop additional internal resources for security, ones that do not necessarily promote a feeling of holding-soothing but that provide various qualities of experience of self that contribute to a sense of personal security. Through various forms of subtle selfobject functioning, the therapist provides the patient with experiences out of which he can, by introjection and identification, develop autonomous capacities not only for feeling soothed and held by means of his own, but also for feeling the reality of his personal qualities, sensing his own self-worth, enjoying his qualities and competences, and affectionately loving himself.

# Five

# The Borderline–Narcissistic Personality Disorder Continuum

The literature defining the features of borderline and narcissistic personality disorders, although complex, has many areas of descriptive agreement. Disagreements arise in discussions of the nature of the psychopathology of these disorders and the treatment implications of these differing formulations.

Some of the major contributors view borderline and narcissistic personality disorders as separate entities. Kohut (1977), for example, sees borderline patients as distinct from those with narcissistic personality disorders and therefore not amenable to the same kind of treatment. Kernberg (1975), in contrast, defines the narcissistic personality disorder as a variety of borderline personality organization. My own clinical work with borderline patients has shown that these patients bear a developmental relationship to those with narcissistic personality disorders—that is, borderline patients, as they improve in therapy, may attain functions and capacities that make them appear similar diagnostically to patients with narcissistic personality disorders.

In this chapter I shall argue the validity and usefulness of conceptualizing patients with borderline and narcissistic personality disorders along a continuum. I hope to demonstrate how, by using the continuum concept, we can increase our diagnostic acumen, clarify the specific vulnerabilities of these patients, and understand the process of change that occurs in psychotherapy. I shall illustrate these formulations with a clinical example of a patient who moved from borderline to narcissistic personality disorder in long-term psychotherapy.

## Diagnostic Considerations

*DSM-III* includes for the first time the diagnostic categories borderline personality disorder and narcissistic personality disorder, and provides operational definitions of each. The *DSM-III* description of borderline personality disorder is consistent with recent clinical research studies (Gunderson and Singer 1975, Gunderson and Kolb 1978, Perry and Klerman 1980) that stress the impulsivity of borderline patients, their intense and unstable relationships, their difficulties with anger, their affect and identity instability, and their propensity to hurt themselves physically. Also described in *DSM-III* are the "chronic feelings of emptiness and boredom" experienced by these patients and their "intolerance of being alone; e.g., [their] frantic efforts to avoid being alone, [as well as being] depressed when alone."

When we compare this description of the borderline personality disorder with that of the narcissistic personality disorder in *DSM-III*, we note certain important differences and similarities. In contrast to the *DSM-III* emphasis on the grandiosity, grandiose fantasies, aloofness, vulnerability to criticism, or indifference toward others of the narcissistic personality disorder, the borderline personality disorder is characterized by intense neediness, lability of affect, and, perhaps most important of all, problems with being alone. Significantly, however, patients in both categories need a response from the other person. Although the patient with a narcissistic personality disorder is more capable of maintaining an aloof indifference, patients with both disorders overidealize, devalue, and manipulate. *DSM-III* may thus be recognizing aspects of two relatively distinct disorders with overlapping areas, perhaps as part of a pragmatic attempt to categorize clinical material about primitive patients.

## Self-Cohesiveness and Selfobject Transference

As we have seen in Chapter 3, the selfobject is needed by the narcissistic personality to maintain a sense of self-worth, by providing a mirroring function or by serving as an object of idealization. Failure of the selfobject function in this regard threatens loss of cohesiveness of the self, generally expressed in such fragmentation experiences as not feeling real, feeling emotionally dull, or lacking in zest and initiative. Such feelings can intensify in regression and are then often manifested in cold, aloof behavior and hypochondriacal preoccupations.

In treatment the therapist as selfobject performs certain fantasied and/or real functions that the patient feels are missing in himself. When selfobject transferences of the mirror or idealizing type emerge and are allowed to flourish, the narcissistic personality is generally able to maintain self-cohesiveness. Fragmentation experiences are usually only transient, resulting from empathic failures of the therapist or severe stresses outside therapy involving losses or threatened losses of selfobject relationships or activities that maintain self-esteem. Even then, these experiences can often be examined in the therapeutic situation without serious disruption. The selfobject transferences of narcissistic patients are thus relatively stable in the face of mild to moderate empathic failures of the therapist. Major failures, often related to countertransference difficulties, may lead to the breakdown of the transference but still not to seriously disruptive experiences for the patient.

A patient who fits the *DSM-III* description of borderline personality disorder may at first be mistaken for a patient with narcissistic personality disorder. At the beginning of therapy, he may form seemingly stable selfobject transferences of the mirror and/or idealizing variety that transiently break down when he experiences empathic failures in the treatment. Gradually, however, or sometimes in a more sudden and dramatic way, and often in spite of the therapist's optimal support and careful attention to possible countertransference difficulties, feelings of dissatisfaction, emptiness, and anger increasingly emerge, usually associated with weekends or other separations from the therapist. Empathic failures of the therapist can then lead to more severe manifestations of loss of self-cohesiveness than Kohut describes for narcissistic personalities—degrees of incoherency or disjointedness of thinking, feelings of loss of integration of body parts, a subjective sense of losing functional control of the self, and concerns about "falling apart." The subsequent breakdown of the borderline patient's tenuously established selfobject transferences can result, in turn, in annihilation panic related to the intensified sense of aloneness the patient experiences once the selfobject bond is broken. The most intense panic follows the regressive loss of evocative memory capacity for the therapist in consequence of rage. The patient, to repeat, often has difficulty remembering the therapist's face between sessions and may even be unable to recognize the therapist while in his presence.

Borderline patients thus differ from narcissistic patients in two critical respects: Their regression involves a greater loss of self-cohesiveness than that experienced by the narcissistic patient, with the ultimate felt threat of annihilation, and a greater potential for serious disruption of the self-object transference. We have already seen, of course, that the basic problem for the borderline patient lies in his relative lack of holding-soothing introjects—his relative incapacity to allay separation anxiety through intrapsychic resources. Whereas the narcissistic patient uses the selfobject to maintain his tenuous sense of self-worth, the borderline patient uses it primarily to provide forms of holding-soothing security, without which he inevitably undergoes a regression through the various stages of loss of self-cohesiveness, culminating in the ultimate threat of self-disintegration. That is to say, in the face of disappointment with or separation from the selfobject, the borderline patient is liable to experience the loss of self-cohesiveness as a prior stage in a process that ends with the felt threat of annihilation. Cohesiveness of the self in borderline personalities is thus as dependent on an equilibrium of holding-soothing as it is on self-worth. The greater loss of self-cohesiveness in regressed borderline patients can be attributed to the fact that failure in the holding-soothing line is developmentally prior to failure in the self-worth line. At the same time, since both lines ultimately contribute to the sense of psychological security, we may fairly speak of them as continuous segments. It is for this reason that issues of self-worth so often become the focus of borderline treatment once the primary issues of holding-soothing security have been resolved: The ultimate development of the autonomous capacity to maintain psychological security awaits the establishment of a solid sense of self-worth. And it is for this same reason that issues of self-worth are often implicated at the very beginning of treatment: It is only with regression that the developmentally prior issues of holding-soothing are reached.

The instability of selfobject transferences in borderline psychotherapy can similarly be traced to the threat of separation anxiety and the developmental failure on which it is based: the patient's imperfectly achieved evocative memory capacity. The formation of stable mirror and idealizing transferences by the narcissistic patient, in contrast, implies a relatively well-developed evocative memory of the therapist and of the patient's relationship with him.

But the instability of the selfobject transferences owes to a perhaps equally significant factor in the therapy of borderline patients. When the borderline patient has allowed himself to become involved in his treatment and has experienced the soothing and comfort of the selfobject as part of the selfobject transferences, he is, as we have seen, more vulnerable to the experiences of aloneness and panic that occur when his anger appears. At the same time, however, his involvement causes him to fear the loss of his separateness, typically in experiences of incorporation or fusion. In contrast, patients with a narcissistic personality disorder can more comfortably maintain varying degrees of merger as part of their selfobject transferences without significant concerns about loss of separateness. Borderline patients intensely fear this loss, which can be conceptualized as a loss of distinct self and object representations or, what is the same thing, the loss of the sense of separate subjective being. Whereas psychotics actually experience the fusion of self and object representations (Jacobson 1964, Kernberg 1975), borderlines largely *fear* its occurrence, and when they do experience it, experience it only transiently. But it remains a fear, akin to Burnham, Gladstone, and Gibson's (1969), need–fear dilemma of schizophrenics. This fear, then, prevents borderline patients from being able to maintain safe, stable selfobject transferences and heightens the disruption that follows experiences of disappointment and anger in treatment. They long for the warmth, holding, and soothing that selfobject transferences provide but fear the threat of loss of separateness that accompanies these experiences.

Borderline patients in psychotherapy will, by definition, regress to some variant of the aloneness problems that are at the core of their disorder, either transiently or in a more profound way. In order for them to make use of the selfobject in the stable manner of the patient with a narcissistic personality disorder, they must first come to terms with their own and the selfobject's psychic and physical survival. They must ultimately learn that their anger neither destroys nor leads to abandonment by the selfobject. Such patients cannot reliably utilize a selfobject as a merged or fused part of themselves until they are certain that the selfobject is dependable both as a selfobject and as a separate entity, and is nondestructible and nonmalignant. To feel that certainty, they must establish within themselves an increasing capacity to maintain a holding introject of the selfobject therapist.

The necessary experience in treatment is one in which the patient's anger, often of momentarily overwhelming intensity, is acknowledged, respected, and understood. Whenever possible this anger can be related to the patient's life story of disappointing, enraging selfobjects as they are reexperienced in the transference. The result is the gradual building up of holding introjects increasingly resilient to regressive loss in the face of the patient's anger. Ultimately, evocative memory capacity for the therapist as a holding, sustaining, soothing figure is established. For some patients this process can occur in months, for others, only in several years. In time, however, the patient may show increasing evidence of a capacity to tolerate separations and empathic failures without disintegrative, annihilatory rage. As a result, for many patients self-destructive behaviors and suicidal fantasies gradually diminish. The building of these new capacities occurs in small increments and can be conceptualized as part of the process of transmuting internalization.

The relationship between borderline and narcissistic personality disorders thus becomes clearer when long-term treatment of borderline patients is studied. That is, borderline patients, once they resolve the issue of aloneness, become more and more like patients with a narcissistic personality disorder. They form increasingly stable selfobject transferences that are more resilient to disruption in the face of disappointments in the therapist and the therapy. Although they may regress to states of aloneness in the middle phases of treatment when their anger becomes too intense, these experiences are short-lived: They reestablish stable selfobject transferences more readily as they progress along the continuum from borderline to narcissistic personality. When borderline patients finally form stable selfobject transferences, they are more likely to idealize the holding aspects of their therapist than are patients with narcissistic personality disorder who have never been borderline.

# Clinical Illustration

I shall illustrate these issues by describing the long-term psychotherapy of a borderline patient that resulted in changes that placed her in the narcissistic personality disorder part of the continuum after four years of treatment.

The patient, Ms. D., was a graduate student in her early thirties when she first sought treatment because of her difficulties in completing her doctoral dissertation. She also wanted help with a long-standing inability to maintain sustained relationships with men. Ms. D. was the youngest of four children of a successful executive who traveled extensively with his wife, who was chronically depressed. When the patient was 2 years old, her parents had a serious automobile accident, necessitating a three-month hospitalization for her mother. Although her father was less seriously injured, he was physically and emotionally unavailable because of his business concerns and the added responsibilities of his wife's hospitalization. During this period Ms. D. and her siblings lived with their grandparents, who were emotionally distant. The patient had a vague memory of these months, seeing herself alone in a gray, cold room; she recalled hearing dimly the voices of unseen persons.

The patient felt that to observers her childhood would appear to have been unremarkable. She struggled to please her teachers, whom she idealized, and fought with her mother about the mother's inability to solve her own problems and about her mother's demands on her. Ms. D. felt her mother was inadequate and ineffectual. She could not stand seeing her mother as helpless, but at the same time she saw herself becoming more and more like her. Ms. D.

had many temper tantrums, which upset the patient and her mother. Her father seemed unavailable; he continued to work long hours and could participate in the family only when intellectual issues were involved. Yet the patient idealized him and felt that many of the warm memories of her childhood occurred at the dinner table when he was home on weekends.

Throughout elementary and high school, the patient had several close girlfriends. She began dating in college and became emotionally involved with a man. She was frightened by the intensity of her feelings of neediness for him, however, and precipitously ended this involvement. After this she avoided heterosexual encounters that could lead to a serious relationship. Although her academic work progressed well, she had no sense of direction, and her feeling of pleasure decreased. She changed her field of graduate study several times, usually at the point when a commitment to a career direction was required. Her fantasies were filled with her idealization of professors and their responses to her as a child who had pleased them by her fine academic work. At the same time she constantly feared that she could not fulfill her fantasies of their expectations, and she often felt panicky at the thought of being abandoned by them. She felt vulnerable and fragile when she realized that it required only a minor disappointment in her work or within a friendship to elicit panic.

The early months of Ms. D.'s twice-weekly psychotherapy were relatively uneventful. The patient established what seemed to be mirror and idealizing selfobject transferences as she told her complicated story. The therapist's summer vacation, which occurred after one month, caused her no difficulty; she used this time to prepare for her fall academic program. She was hopeful about her therapy and confident that the therapist could aid her in solving her difficulties.

When the sessions resumed, Ms. D.'s hopefulness continued at first. As her graduate studies required more effort, however, she became increasingly concerned that she would be unable to please her professors. She began to feel empty and panicky, feelings that were most pronounced on weekends. During the next several months these feelings intensified; the patient had a persistent fantasy that she was like a small child who wished and needed to be held but was being abandoned. As her panic states kept recurring, she felt more and more hopeless and empty.

Ms. D. gradually acknowledged, with much fear, that she felt furious at her therapist. Because anger was totally unacceptable to her, she felt guilty and worthless and believed she would be punished. It seemed inconceivable to her that her therapist would tolerate anyone who ever felt any anger toward him. Her fury increased, accompanied by overwhelming guilt. At times when she felt she needed more support, she experienced the therapy as a situation of inadequate holding. During some sessions the patient would scream in a rage and then pound her fists against her head or hit her head against the wall. At the height of her rage, she would leave her sessions frightened that she could not remember the therapist.

The patient used the therapist's offer of additional sessions and his availability by phone to help her with increasingly frequent experiences of panic between sessions, when she felt that he no longer existed or that she had "stomped" him to death in her mind while in a rage at him. Although her calls were brief and allowed her to tolerate the time between sessions better, hospitalization was required when she became seriously suicidal just before his vacation. She was able to resume out-patient treatment on his return.

These episodes of disappointment, rage, panic, and loss of the ability to remember the therapist between sessions continued intermittently over two years. As they gradually diminished, the patient stated that she more readily felt held and supported by the therapist and viewed him as someone she admired who could help her. A major change occurred after the therapist's vacation at the beginning of the fourth year of therapy. The patient stated that she clearly missed him for the first time, that is, she felt consistent sadness and longing instead of panic and abandonment. Concomitantly, she talked about warm memories of shared experiences with her mother, in contrast to the predominantly negative, angry memories of her mother that had filled the early years of treatment.

By the end of the fourth year of treatment, the patient had no further episodes of unbearable rage followed by panic and aloneness. The predominant issues in therapy related to an exploration of her serious self-worth problems and her increasing ability to examine these issues, both as they appeared through disappointments in her life and in the transference, in which she idealized the therapist and used mirroring and validating responses. She gradually came to feel more comfortable with her anger at the therapist for his real or fantasized failures in his responses to her, without losing the sense of his support more than momentarily during a specific session.

### DISCUSSION

Ms. D.'s case history illustrates aspects of the border-line–narcissistic personality disorder continuum. Specifically, after four years this patient was able to resolve issues

of borderline aloneness and move into the narcissistic personality disorder part of the continuum, in which she could
maintain relatively stable selfobject transferences and self-
cohesiveness. During this process she developed evocative
memory for her therapist that was resistant to regression.
She also became increasingly able to bear ambivalence
toward her therapist and others, while concentrating in
therapy primarily on issues of her vulnerable self-worth.

# Six

# The Myth of the Alliance

In clinical work with borderline patients, we are frequently impressed with the rapid breakdown of what seems to be a tenuous, or sometimes even more solid, alliance. Desperate borderline aloneness can emerge when unbearable affects appear in the therapy or when the therapist makes a response that is unempathic or perhaps incorrect. Similarly, when we examine the narcissistic personality disorders with their stable selfobject transferences, we can ask whether a therapeutic alliance exists or whether these primitive transferences themselves allow the patient to be sustained in the treatment. Although we invoke concepts of alliance and make statements about building alliance, it seems probable that the empathic support and optimal frustration offered by the therapist provide the empathic framework that the patient needs in order to sustain himself with a selfobject transference; the therapist can mistake this stable transference for an alliance.

In this chapter I shall delineate a developmental sequence that culminates in the patient's capacity to form a therapeutic alliance. I hope thereby to expand our understanding of the concepts of transference, real relationship, and alliance in all patients, based upon examination of the recent literature about borderline and narcissistic personality disorders and clinical experiences with them. In particular, I shall be considering the primitive or selfobject transferences (Kohut 1977) these patients form and their relationship to the evolving capacity to observe and utilize the objective qualities of the therapist ultimately to develop a mature therapeutic alliance that can withstand the vicissitudes of intense affects, impulses, wishes, and conflicts. I shall then discuss the relationship of these selfobject transferences to the analysis of all patients and the formation of the usual neurotic dyadic and triadic transferences.

The concepts of alliance, transference, selfobject transference, and real relationship are complex, interrelated, and often confusing. It is generally acknowledged that alliances derive from transference and relate to certain successful childhood experiences and developmental achievements, which obviously include relationships with people, both past and present. Because the separation of these concepts is important theoretically and clinically, I shall define the ways in which I shall use some of these terms.

## Definitions

Transference is the experiencing of affects, wishes, fantasies, attitudes, and defenses toward a person in the present that were originally experienced in a past relationship to a significant figure in childhood (Greenson 1965). As a displacement of issues from old relationships to present ones, transference is always inappropriate to the present. It can also be conceived as a projection of inner or internalized or partially internalized superego (Zetzel 1956), ego ideal, id, or ego aspects onto the present person. Selfobject transferences are transferences in which the therapist and patient are variably fused along a complex continuum in which the therapist performs certain functions for the patient that are absent in the patient. The therapist's performance of these functions is necessary for the patient to feel whole and complete, while experiencing these therapist functions as part of himself. As defined by Kohut (1971, 1977), the narcissistic patient needs the therapist's mirroring responses and his acceptance of the patient's idealization. The borderline patient, as we have seen, needs the therapist to perform holding-soothing functions. Dyadic and triadic transferences are those transferences most often found in neurotic patients and are usually related to the transferences in the transference neurosis. They imply solid self and object differentiation as well as minimal use of projection and projective identification such that these defenses do not significantly interfere with reality testing. The further distinctions between selfobject transferences and dyadic-triadic transferences will be discussed later.

I shall use alliance in the usual sense of Zetzel's (1956) therapeutic alliance and Greenson's (1965) working alliance as derived from Sterba (1934), an alliance between the analyzing ego of the therapist and the patient's reasonable ego. It involves mutuality, collaboration, and the mature aspects of two individuals working together to understand something and to resolve a problem. Although it derives from and relates to earlier kinds of relationships that can be considered precursors or aspects of alliance, my utilization of the term stresses mature collaboration.

By real relationship I am referring to the actual relationship between patient and therapist, which is based upon the patient's perception of the objective attributes of the therapist as they are distinguished from transference. To perceive the real attributes of the therapist, the patient must have achieved a significant degree of self and object differentiation and must not utilize projection and projective identification to an extent that they obscure the therapist's objective attributes. The real relationship is also referred to as the personal relationship between patient and therapist (A. Freud 1954, Lipton 1977). The personal relationship is generally used to mean the way the therapist utilizes his personality and human qualities to relate to his patient, and includes such qualities as his flexibility, warmth, and openness. For this personal relationship to be synonymous with the real relationship in the patient's eyes, the patient should have achieved sufficient self and object differentiation and concomitant capacity to test reality to perceive this personal relationship in objective terms, that is, as separate from transference. The real relationship must also be distinguished from such concepts as "the therapist's being more real." The latter is often used to describe issues such as the amount of activity by the therapist and his sharing of personal information in response to his perception of the patient's needs or demands. It may or may not coincide with the patient's objective perceptions of this activity at the moment or at some other time, again based upon the degree of the patient's self and object differentiation and uses of projection and projective identification at the moment, which in part may be determined by the intensity of the transference.

## The Transference-Alliance Literature

Zetzel (1956) is credited by Greenson (1965) with introducing the term therapeutic alliance into the psychoanalytic literature, although the alliance concept was implicit in the work of others. Fenichel (1941) describes the "rational transference," and Stone (1961) writes about the "mature transference." Greenson's (1965) working alliance is similar to Zetzel's but emphasizes the patient's capacity to work in the psychoanalytic situation.

Friedman (1969), in his scholarly discussion of the therapeutic alliance, delineates the complexities and paradoxes in Freud's development of the concept of transference and its link to the idea of alliance. Freud (1910a, 1910b, 1912, 1913) was aware that transference was not only a resistance, but also a helpful bond in keeping the patient in treatment. He attempted to resolve the contradiction by ascribing the resistance to negative feelings and defenses against unconscious erotic feelings toward the analyst. The positive bond was strengthened by the patients "conscious" and "unobjectionable" feelings.

The interrelationship of transference as a resistance to treatment and transference as an ally of the therapist and motivating force in treatment is a theme throughout Freud's writing, as Friedman describes. Freud, in his last attempts to address the transference and alliance dilemma (1937), utilizes the structural theory. He writes of "an alliance with the ego of the patient to subdue certain uncontrolled parts of his id, i.e., to include them in the synthesis of the ego" (p. 235), and states that the positive transference "is the patient's strongest motive for the patient's taking a share in the joint work of analysis" (p. 233). Here, too, transference and alliance seem inextricably intermeshed.

In all this work, Freud rarely discussed the real relationship between patient and analyst. Lipton (1977) attributes this omission to the fact that Freud was describing technique and, for example, the neutrality required in it. The personal relationship was obviously present and obviously important, as Freud's notes of his work with the Rat Man (1909) reveal, and as confirmed by reports from Freud's former analysands (Lipton 1977).

Perhaps we can sort out some elements in the use of transference and alliance in Freud's technique papers by examining the various functions of transference and alliance in therapy and the therapist's and patient's different uses of them. The positive transference, which keeps the patient in treatment, is primarily experienced by the patient as something he feels when he thinks about the therapist or is with him. The alliance, in contrast, is utilized by the therapist to help the patient look at something, including the experience of transference (P. G. Myerson, personal communication, 1978), and is felt by the patient as an awareness that the therapist's actions are motivated by the patient's best interests (Myerson 1964). The alliance aspects support looking, reflecting, examining, and insight. The transference supports attachment and emotional involvement. However, a careful examination of these distinctions clinically can sometimes reveal the lack of a clear difference between them: Sometimes what appears to be an alliance is compliance on the part of the patient; the patient may wish to please the therapist in order to get gratification or avoid fantasied punishment—in short, the transference can be confused with the alliance (Greenson 1965; P. G. Myerson, personal communication, 1978).

In a recent paper Gutheil and Havens (1979) draw heavily upon Friedman's work to delineate transference and alliance concepts. Utilizing Friedman's descriptions they categorize many varieties of alliance. Although they tend to allow a blurring between transference and alliance to remain, they provide an interesting lead into new territory. They attempt to validate their complex categorization of forms of alliance by seeing whether they can apply their categories to Kohut's writing, using one of his major works, *The Analysis of the Self* (1971). They believe that Kohut himself confuses transference and alliance; Kohut emphasizes that stability in analysis occurs when the narcissistic (1971) or selfobject (1977) transferences that develop in narcissistic personality disorders are allowed to emerge through the therapist's empathic understanding. These transferences especially flourish when there are no intrusive alliance-building statements or specifically defined countertransference difficulties that can disrupt their appearance and solidification. Once these selfobject transferences are established in the narcissistic personality disorder, Kohut states, the framework for a stable clinical analyzable situation exists.

As Gutheil and Havens point out, however, Kohut also speaks of the alliance in narcissistic personality disorders in a statement that is reminiscent of Sterba:

> The observing segment of the personality of the analysand which, in cooperation with the analyst, has actively shouldered the task of analyzing, is not, in essence, different in analyzable narcissistic disorders from that found in analyzable transference neuroses. In both types of cases an adequate area of realistic cooperation derived from positive experiences in childhood (in the object-cathected *and* narcissistic realm) is the precondition for the analysand's maintenance of the therapeutic split of the ego and for that fondness for the analyst which assures the maintenance of a sufficient trust in the processes and goals of analysis during stressful periods (Kohut 1971, p. 207).

Although the stable analytic situation in the treatment of narcissistic personality disorders arises from the emergence of the selfobject transferences, Kohut feels that these patients also have the capacity for realistic cooperation with the analyst, that is, they form alliances as well as selfobject transferences.

The problem with Kohut's statement lies in its lack of validation based upon clinical experience. In psychotherapeutic work with narcissistic personality disorders, we can observe that a stable clinical situation is present once the selfobject transferences emerge, but we find rational cooperation and an observing ego tenuous and easily lost. As Kohut himself points out, an empathic failure can rupture this rational bond to a degree not present in neurotic patients. Thus, patients with narcissistic personality disorders are capable of the capacities defined by Kohut to a relatively large extent once the selfobject transferences are firmly established and if not stressed too greatly by serious empathic failures or countertransference difficulties. Despite Kohut's inconsistencies about the interrelationship between selfobject transference and alliance, as outlined by Gutheil and Havens, his descriptions of the stabilizing effects of selfobject transferences in the treatment of narcissistic personality disorders can provide the link in our discussion of the relationship of these transferences to other transferences, the real relationship with the therapist, and alliance formation.

## Selfobject Transferences and Transference Neurosis

Kohut's selfobject transference concept, which he developed in his work with narcissistic personality disorders and which I have extended to borderline patients, is related to concepts utilized by other workers, especially when they describe the early phases of treatment of all patients. As Fleming (1972) states, the analytic situation is designed to shift the balance in the usual sources of comfort for a patient. All patients early in treatment tend to feel alone and wish to return to the security of the early mother–child relationship. The holding environment concepts of Winnicott (1960) refer to these same wishes and needs. Fleming (1972, 1975) stresses Mahler's (1968) symbiosis concepts as crucial in the early treatment situation. Erikson's (1959) basic trust concepts, Gitelson's (1962) discussion of the diatrophic function of the analyst, and Stone's (1961) descriptions of the "mother associated with intimate bodily care" are also related to the special issues of the early phases of treatment. Although these workers are using a variety of theoretical models and terms, I believe they are referring to a clinical situation early in the treatment of analyzable neurotic patients in which transferences emerge that may at times be indistinguishable from Kohut's selfobject transferences. In fact, a major task of the therapist or analyst in the early phases of treatment of all patients may be that of providing the setting, support, and clarifications and interpretive help that allow these selfobject transferences to emerge. The development of these selfobject transferences may coincide with the therapist's sense that the patient is "settling down" in treatment and is comfortable enough to be able to begin working collaboratively.

Obviously, the type of selfobject transference is largely determined by the specific needs of the patient. For this reason, the selfobject transferences that are present in neurotic patients may not be visible under ordinary circumstances. They may be established silently and unobtrusively in the therapeutic situation, in part through the consistency, reliability, and understanding that the therapist supplies from the beginning of treatment. The issues that are central to the selfobject transferences, that is, issues of self-worth and holding-soothing, are usually not major unresolved issues for neurotics. Thus, neurotic patients do not generally return to these issues for further resolution as part of the unfolding transferences. Instead, these selfobject transferences provide the silent, stable basis for work on the more unsettled issues that make up the conflicts of the transference neurosis of many readily treatable neurotic patients.

The therapist's recognition of these silent selfobject transferences, however, may be important for neurotic patients in at least two circumstances (D. H. Buie, personal communication, 1979): (1) a retreat by some patients to these selfobject transference issues as a defense against the onslaughts of a confronting therapist, and (2) difficulties in termination that may be related to unanalyzed selfobject transference issues that emerge during the termination process. When repeatedly confronted by a therapist with formulations that are beyond the patient's capacity to acknowledge at the time, or that may even be incorrect, the patient can regress defensively in a way related to Winnicott's (1960) descriptions of a false self. Under these circumstances an idealizing selfobject transference may be one of the ways the patient can protect himself from his therapist's intrusiveness, while sacrificing opportunities for constructive psychotherapeutic work. During termination it is possible that some of the expected reappearance of old symptoms and conflicts may also be related to unanalyzed selfobject transference issues that only now emerge when the selfobject bond between patient and therapist is about to be severed. Unless these are identified and examined, an opportunity for crucial therapeutic work can be lost. Finally, it is important to recognize that there is a large group of neurotic patients who require work at many points in their treatment on selfobject as well as dyadic-triadic issues. These patients have clearly advanced into the neurotic levels of unresolved conflict that becomes manifest in the transference neurosis. Yet there are sufficient unsettled earlier issues that require work on the level of selfobject as well as later transferences as the patient's material shifts from these different levels. Significant unfinished work can result from a focus on one rather than multiple levels of transference.

## Relationship of Selfobject, Dyadic, and Triadic Transferences to Alliance

In contrast to the dyadic and triadic transferences, the selfobject transferences usually imply some degree of fusion of patient and therapist. Still, if we examine the full spectrum of selfobject transferences as Kohut (1971, 1977) defines them, we see that they include both the most primitive varieties, with significant degrees of merger, and more differentiated ones that include complete separateness of patient and therapist. For example, "the mirror transference in the narrower sense" is a variety of selfobject transference that Kohut describes as similar to the twinkle in the mother's eye as she admires her child. This form of selfobject transference, then, is one in which an interaction between two separate people is occurring. The selfobject transferences in which the patient and therapist are separate people, and which may include mirroring as well as idealizing varieties, seem to be a form of dyadic transference seen in neurotic patients. There thus appears to be a point in the continuum between selfobject and neurotic transferences in which there is no clear distinction between them—in which there is complete separateness of patient and therapist. At that point the transference may be said to be dyadic. Of course, not every dyadic transference is a more differentiated selfobject transference. Selfobject transferences by definition are related to issues of sustenance, grandiosity, and idealization. Therefore, they would not include dyadic transferences seen in neurotics that focus on, for example, struggles over control and power in relationship to the therapist as mother or father in the transference. But they would include the kind of silent transferences often present in neurotic patients that support emotional involvement with the therapist—the so-called positive transference.

Another quality that seems to distinguish selfobject and dyadic-triadic transferences is the patients' passivity or activity in these transferences (P. G. Myerson, personal communication, 1979). In the selfobject transferences patients more often wish to be held, fed, admired, and passively comforted, in contrast to the more active, assertive wishes and fantasies associated with the dyadic-triadic transferences. When frustrated or disappointed within the selfobject transferences, however, patients do experience an active anger that can be associated with destructive fantasies as well as with experiences of fragmentation.

## The Real Relationship

Discussions about the real relationship in psychoanalysis and psychotherapy tend to occur most often among clinicians who work with borderline and narcissistic personality disorder patients. The emergence of several relevant issues in the treatment of these patients may help explain the interest in the real relationship: (1) This group of patients may complain with intensity that they need something more than the therapist is giving. (2) They may state specifically that the therapist is not real to them and ask or demand to know details about his life, or demand to have an extra-therapeutic relationship in order to feel that the therapist is "real." (3) The therapist in working with these patients may feel both empathically and theoretically that these patients need something more than an approach that emphasizes clarification and interpretation.

These issues raise a major difficulty in discussing the real relationship. A patient demanding more from his therapist may be making a statement about intense transference longings, anger, or disappointments. Or the patient may be revealing a developmental failure on the basis of which he feels incomplete and requires some response to establish the situation that remedies this feeling, at least temporarily. At the same time, the patient may be pointing to an actual deficiency in a therapist who is failing to provide the necessary response either to the transference demand or to the requirements for a selfobject relationship that the patient needs in order to work with the therapist. If we use the term personal relationship to refer to the qualities of the therapist that objectively exist and that become a part of his interaction with the patient which the patient perceives objectively, we can more clearly separate transference issues from issues of the real relationship.

Borderline and narcissistic personalities can establish both selfobject and dyadic-triadic transferences, although the intense transference demands of these patients usually relate to the failure of selfobject transferences to be established or maintained. The demands by the patient for the therapist to be more real often refer to these selfobject transference failures or breakdowns. If the therapist responds to these intense transference requests, for example, for more facts about the therapist, by sharing more about himself, a variety of results could occur. If the therapist's responses coincidentally help to establish or reestablish the selfobject transferences, the patient may become more comfortable and work more effectively in the therapy. On the other hand, when the therapist shares more about himself without clarifying or interpreting the transference, he may be felt unconsciously by the patient to be missing the essence of the patient's transference difficulties, and thus providing another disappointment; this disappointment can be followed by an angry escalation of demands for even more from the therapist. Thus, the correct assessment of the patient's demands may be crucial; if the issue is the breakdown of selfobject transferences, the work should involve clarification and interpretation; it may also include efforts to clarify distortions in the personal relationship between patient and therapist.

A paradox exists, especially with borderline and narcissistic personalities, in our understanding of the personal relationship between patient and therapist and the patient's utilization of this personal relationship to facilitate the therapeutic work. At the beginning of treatment these patients often require an awareness of the person and personality of the therapist as someone appropriately interested, caring, warm, and wishing to be helpful in order to establish the selfobject transferences that stabilize the treatment and make optimal therapeutic work possible. Yet these same patients may have minimal capacities to define and observe these objective attributes in the therapist and utilize them for internalizations. The paradox relates to the fact that many of these patients have relatively secure capacities to see a relationship objectively only when the selfobject transferences are firmly established, that is, when they have regained functions previously present. These functions are transiently lost in the regression that often brings them into treatment, and that often involves a loss of a selfobject relationship or a loss of an activity that maintains self-worth. It requires the stability of the established selfobject transferences to reverse the transiently lost ability to observe clearly and define the personal qualities of the therapist. That is, the firmly established selfobject transferences, usually involving some degree of merger, allow the patient to regain concomitant capacities to appreciate the separateness of the therapist and the many areas of the patient's own separateness, which were *transiently* lost in the regression that usually leads these patients to seek treatment (and lost to a greater extent by borderline patients than by narcissistic patients as a general rule). With this appreciation, the patient can also begin to internalize objective qualities of the therapist that are missing in himself and idealized aspects projected onto the therapist as part of the selfobject transference. Patients with a borderline personality disorder, because of their occasionally tenuous self and object differentiation and primitive avoidance defenses that become most manifest as intense affects emerge, may have the most difficulty in perceiving and utilizing the objective qualities of the therapist. They therefore may require greater activity from the therapist in his demonstration of his willingness to clarify, explain, be helpful, and meet the patient's level of regression (P. G. Myerson 1964, 1976; personal communication, 1979). In making this statement, I am not minimizing the importance of an interpretive approach that focuses on transference and reconstruction. Nor am I unaware of the dangers of activity that may be perceived by the patient as smothering, engulfing, or seductive, or that may be a maneuver by the therapist to avoid the anger that the patient may be experiencing. Still, the therapist's goal is to foster a therapeutic situation in which the selfobject transferences can emerge and their pathological aspects can be interpreted. To achieve this goal, the possible excessive gratification brought about by the therapist's activity must be weighed against the patient's limited capacity to tolerate deprivation at any specific moment.

In psychotherapeutic work with neurotic patients, the silent selfobject transferences are more readily established in the average expectable therapeutic environment. Neurotic patients can tolerate a wider range of styles and personalities in the therapist as part of their personal relationship with him, although there is an optimal spectrum within the wider range. They can also more readily perceive the objective qualities of the therapist and utilize these objective qualities therapeutically after the selfobject transferences and transference neurosis flourish.

## The Emerging Therapeutic Alliance

We can now discuss the relevance of all these considerations to the "myth of the alliance" with borderline patients. As Friedman (1969) and A. Ornstein (1975, quoted by Berkowitz 1977) note, the requirement that a patient establish or have the capacity to establish a therapeutic alliance at the beginning of therapy is the request for a capacity that is the end result of a successful therapy. In fact, the demand for an alliance may tax an already tenuous sense of psychological security in the patient. Yet clinically we attempt to assess such alliance potential in our diagnostic evaluations. If a patient responds with a confirmatory nod and amplification to a clarification that we present to the patient as something we can look at together, how can we know whether the patient feels supported by the empathic correctness of the statement or by its appeal to collaboration? Even if he responds to the "we" aspect of the statement, what does the "we" mean to him? Is it the collaboration of two separate people, or does he hear the "we" to mean the partial fusion of two people, that is, a statement supporting the formation of a selfobject transference?

My own work with primitive patients suggests that the "we" invoked by the therapist often makes the therapist more comfortable but is effective only when it coincides with the patient's feeling sustained through a selfobject transference. The patient usually does not experience the working collaboration; instead, he is held in the therapy by feeling supported, soothed, and understood. The therapist's activities in this regard help to create the selfobject transference. But they do not establish a therapeutic alliance, only its selfobject precursors, which ultimately can be internalized slowly as the primitive transferences are resolved and neurotic transferences become more solidly established. At the point that the patient is capable of a solid therapeutic alliance, that patient no longer has a borderline or narcissistic personality disorder; in fact, he is well within the neurotic spectrum and approaching the end of therapy.

The therapeutic alliance in its mature, stable form is thus usually only present in a later stage of treatment, although precursors or unstable forms of it may be visible earlier. The therapeutic alliance derives from the resolutions of early (selfobject) and later (dyadic-triadic) transferences, and requires the patient's capacity to separate the personal relationship with the therapist from the transference. Internalizations that occur through resolution of the selfobject and neurotic transferences, which include internalizations of projections of the inner world or introjects onto the therapist, are part of this process that leads to the patient's increasing capacity to form a therapeutic alliance.

For all these reasons, there are dangers in using alliance-building statements at times when the alliance is not viable developmentally for the patient at a particular stage in therapy. These statements can be used to obscure the fact that the therapist is not empathically in touch with his patient and is appealing to reason when he does not understand the patient, leading to disruptions of the selfobject transference, as the following vignette suggests.

A 35-year-old single woman who sought therapy for chronic depression and inability to maintain relationships with men was regarded by both her therapist and his supervisor as someone with a hysterical character problem. After nearly a year of twice-weekly psychotherapy, the patient remained essentially unchanged and felt that she was making little progress. The therapist focused his work on her disappointment in her relationship with her father and competitive feelings toward her mother. He also stressed the collaborative nature of their work and emphasized frequently that the two of them were looking at or could look at certain issues and feelings together.

Following one of these exhortations about collaboration, the patient looked her therapist squarely in the eye and said, "Don't give me any more of that 'we' crap!" Although the therapist was momentarily stunned, he had no adequate response or explanation. It was only after careful review of his work with the patient that he concluded that he had been treating someone with a narcissistic personality disorder as a person with a neurotic character problem. His lack of understanding of the nature of the patient's despair and developmental difficulties was perceived by the patient as the therapist's empathic failure. Under those circumstances there was little to sustain the patient except for her perception that the therapist was occasionally empathically correct and struggled to understand her; nothing suggesting a therapeutic alliance, however, was ever present with her.

To summarize, I believe that a sequence occurs in the successful therapy of primitive patients: (1) the establishment of stable selfobject transferences that sustain them,

(2) the increasing capacity to appreciate the therapist as a real and separate person, and (3) the gradual ability to ally themselves with the therapist in the service of accomplishing work.

Using these formulations, the therapist has as a major task the clarification of where the patient lies in this continuum, what causes the patient's fluctuations within it, and what responses by the therapist will solidify the patient's achievements as he advances along it. Thus, the primitive patient's dissatisfaction that the therapist is not real to him may be viewed as the patient's failure to establish a sustaining selfobject transference at that moment. The therapist's formulations and empathic understanding determine his responses at different times and are specifically related to clarification or interpretation that addresses the appropriate point of the developmental sequence.

# Seven

# Uses of Confrontation

On the basis of my clinical work, I have become convinced that confrontation is useful in treating all borderline patients and essential to the progress of some. In this chapter I hope to convey what I have learned about the uses of confrontation. In the process I shall be discussing in some detail the characteristic defenses of borderline patients, and further clarifying their differences from narcissistic patients.

## Definition of Confrontation

No single definition of "confrontation" is widely accepted, and some disagreements are the result of covert differences in the way the term is technically defined. Some problems also arise from the confusion of the technical meaning of confrontation with some of the meanings given in standard dictionaries. "To stand facing . . . in challenge, defiance, opposition" is one such meaning (*Webster's New World Dictionary*, 1960). This confusion, also covert, leads to implications that, in confronting, the therapist necessarily endangers his selfobject relationship with the patient.

Another source of confusion arises from the use of clinical examples in teaching and writing about confrontation. These examples are complex. The specific confrontation is usually artfully integrated with other maneuvers, such as clarification or interpretation, and with the affects and personal style of the therapist. Separating out that which constitutes the confrontation can be quite difficult, and discussions about it can imperceptibly shade and shift into the pros and cons of the other elements, any of which may come to be mistaken for facets of confrontation.

In response to these problems, I have attempted to work out a definition. I approach it through the teachings and writings of Khantzian, Dalsimer, and Semrad (1969), Semrad (1954, 1968, 1969), Murray (1964, 1973), and E. Bibring (1954). Semrad's work concerned psychotic and borderline patients. He emphasized their reliance on certain defenses—denial, projection, and distortion—that he termed the "avoidance devices." These defenses operate to keep conscious and preconscious experiences out of awareness. As such, they are to be differentiated from other defenses, such as repression, that serve to keep experiences not only out of awareness but also unconscious. To help patients become aware of avoided painful feelings, impulses, and experiences, Semrad used a combination of support and pressure. The support makes distress more bearable and thus lessens the need for avoidance. The pressure against avoidance is then applied directly and actively, usually by a series of questions along with various countermoves in response to the patient's evasions.

Murray (1964) wrote about work with borderline and neurotic patients who exhibit considerable regression to the pregenital level. An infantile, narcissistic entitlement to life on their terms is often a major force behind the resistance of these patients to clarifications, interpretations, and acceptance of the real world. Even after clarifications and interpretations have been thoroughly established, this kind of patient tries to maintain his pleasurable pregenital world by avoiding acknowledgment of what he now consciously knows. In the setting of support, Murray, like Semrad, applied pressure in various forms (surprise, humor, forceful manner) against these avoidances. Murray referred to this technique as "confrontation." It seems to us appropriate to apply the same term to Semrad's technique.

In his classic paper, E. Bibring (1954) listed five groups of basic techniques used in all psychotherapies. His categorization continues to be useful, although it was derived primarily from work with neurotic patients. He described a central technique, interpretation, for working with those defenses that keep material unconscious. But he included no method for working with defenses that simply prevent awareness of material that is already available in consciousness—that is, preconscious or conscious. One of Bibring's techniques, clarification, does deal with preconscious or conscious material—as a method for bringing into awareness or sharpening awareness of behavior patterns—but Bibring specified that the patient *does not resist acknowledging that which is clarified.* He accepts it readily. It is because avoidance devices are used so prominently by psychotic, borderline, and pregenitally regressed neurotic patients, and because confrontation, as employed by Semrad and Murray, is specifically designed to deal with these defenses, that I believe that confrontation should be added to Bibring's categories of techniques.

Accordingly, I would define confrontation as follows: Confrontation is a technique designed to gain a patient's attention to inner experiences or perceptions of outer reality of which he is conscious or is about to be made conscious. Its specific purpose is to counter resistances to recognizing what is, in fact, available to awareness or about to be made available through clarification or interpretation. Although the purpose of confrontation is not to induce or force change in the patient's attitudes, decisions, or conduct, my definition resembles that of Myerson (1973) in that I believe confrontation to involve the use of force. My definition is, in fact, built upon his. The difference is that I am more explicit about the purposes for which the force is and is not to be employed.

Confrontation can be used in combination with other of the basic techniques. For example, when a patient can be expected to mobilize denial against a clarification that he otherwise would be able to grasp, the therapist may combine the clarification with a confrontation. Rather than deliver the clarification as a simple statement, the therapist may try to capture the patient's attention at the same time, perhaps by using a loud voice, an expletive, or an unusual phrase.

This definition of confrontation involves differentiating it especially from two of the techniques listed by Bibring (1954): suggestion and manipulation. Some clinical vignettes offered as examples of confrontation are, in fact, more accurately described by Bibring's accounts of these two techniques. They amount to forcefully executed suggestions or manipulations. Limit setting is one such maneuver. Often it is presented as a confrontation when it is well subsumed under the category of manipulation.

## Description of Confrontation

There are, of course, very many methods used by patients for avoiding awareness of that which is consciously available. Suppression, denial, projection, and distortion are the ones classically described. Diversion through activity, superficial acknowledgment followed by changing the subject, rationalization, and intellectualization are a few more of the ways to avoid awareness. Any complete discussion of the topic of avoidance would carry us beyond the scope of this chapter. A. Freud (1936), Jacobson (1957), Bibring, Dwyer, Huntington, and Valenstein (1961), Lewin (1950), Vaillant (1971), and Semrad (1968, 1969) are among the authors contributing to my understanding of this subject.

I should, however, make a few more comments describing the technique of confrontation. Occasionally the verbal content of a confrontation is itself sufficient to claim the patient's attention. More frequently the manner of delivery is the effective agent. Surprise, humor, an unusual choice of words, or an emphatic delivery may capture the patient's awareness. Or the therapist may choose to use a show of personal feelings, such as obvious person-to-person caring, sadness, frustration, or anger. Essentially, any departure from the usual tone or format can be used in the service of confrontation.

A caveat for the therapist was issued by Murray (1973) and Myerson (1973). It is specific for confrontations that involve expression of the therapist's feelings: The therapist's feelings must always be experienced as in the patient's behalf. This is especially true of anger. Otherwise the therapist violates his unspoken commitment to the selfobject relationship. Such violation constitutes a narcissistically based power play in the form of antitherapeutic suggestion or manipulation.

## Libidinal Drives, Aggressive Drives, and Attendant Feelings

As we have seen, the borderline patient's psychopathology is founded on one fundamental belief: that he is, or will be, abandoned. He believes it because internalization of basic mother–infant caring is incomplete. His fundamental feeling is terror of utter aloneness, a condition that feels to him like annihilation. Concomitant and derivative experiences are emptiness, hunger, and coldness, within and without.

Abandonment by the person needed to sustain life— mother or her surrogate—is not simply terrifying; it is enraging. This rage may be simply destructive, but more often it is experienced along with desperate efforts to obtain the needed person permanently. This experience occurs in the mode of the infant at the oral level. The patient urgently, savagely, wants to kill that person, eat him, be eaten by him, or gain skin-to-skin contact to the extreme of merging through bodily absorption—either absorbing or being absorbed. This oral, raging acquisitiveness, mobilized in response to abandonment, brings in its wake further difficulties. Destroying his needed object mobilizes primitive guilt; it also threatens him again with helpless aloneness. He may attempt to save the object from his destructive urges by withdrawal. But that, too, threatens intolerable aloneness. He can call upon projection to deal with his rage. But projecting the rage onto another object now makes that object a dreaded source of danger. Once again the patient seeks self-protection by distancing and withdrawal, and again he faces the state of aloneness.

## Methods of Defense

I have already described two of the borderline patient's methods of defense. One is projection of his oral destructiveness. By projecting, he achieves only the partial relief offered by externalizing; he still feels in danger, but now from without rather than from within. Related to this type of projection is projective identification, which includes projection plus the need to control the object in order to avoid the projected danger (Kernberg 1967). The other defense is mobilization of rage in the service of defense against expected abandonment or oral attack. This defense is very primitive, derived more from the id than from the ego. As such, it constitutes an impulse that is nearly as frightening to the patient as the threats against which it defends.

Kernberg (1967) elucidates the borderline patient's use of the splitting of his internal objects in an effort to deal with intense ambivalence. These patients also employ displacement and hostility against the self. A variety of other defenses, including repression, are also available to them. In my opinion, however, Semrad (1968) was correct in emphasizing the avoidance devices as these patients' main line of defense. Specific methods of avoidance, as he listed them are denial, distortion, and projection; they are put into operation against conscious content in an effort to keep it out of awareness. I would add yet another method: avoidance by taking action.

Having already described the borderline patient's use of projection, I can turn now to denial, distortion, and avoidance by taking action. Denial, as defined by Jacobson (1957) and Bibring, Dwyer, Huntington, and Valenstein (1961), may be employed lightly or may be used massively, to the point that the patient is unaware of any feeling or any impulse. Much the same can be said of distortion, whereby the patient not only denies inner or outer reality but also substitutes a fantasy version to suit his defensive purposes. Denial and distortion carry two serious defects. One is that they are brittle. When threatened with facing what he avoids, the patient can intensify his denial or distortion, but he is likely to become desperate in doing so. And when the defense is cracked, it can too readily give way altogether.

The other defect is that these defenses heavily obfuscate reality.

Avoidance can also be achieved by discharging impulses and feelings through the medium of action. The action may be a more or less neutral form of outlet or it may express, at least in part, the nature of the feelings or impulses that the patient does not wish to acknowledge. Because it always involves taking action without understanding, more or less blindly, this method of avoidance is hazardous. Through it the patient allows himself action that is directly destructive or places him in danger. Avoidance through action is commonly used along with massive denial of feelings, so that the patient may be in the especially dangerous situation of discharging impulses like an automaton, feeling nothing at all and even being utterly unaware of the nature and consequences of his acts. This problem will be discussed further in a later section.

On the basis of this description, we can make three general statements about the borderline patient's defenses: (1) They are often maintained at the sacrifice of being in touch with reality, which is a far greater sacrifice than that involved with higher level defenses; (2) they tend to be inadequate to maintain equilibrium, to be brittle, and to be in themselves a source of distress; and (3) they can place the patient in danger.

# The Need for Confrontation in Treating Borderline Patients

## CONFRONTATION IN EVERYDAY TREATMENT

Intensity and chaos characterize life as experienced at the borderline level. Most borderline patients occasionally experience their lives almost solely at that level, unmodified by more mature attainments. But usually their borderline problems are simply interwoven into the music of everyday life, sometimes in counterpoint and sometimes in harmony with healthier themes and rhythms. At times the problems swell to dominate the composition; at other times they are heard only softly in the background.

Most therapy hours are, then, characterized by steady, undramatic work by therapist and patient. Is confrontation needed, or useful, during these hours? In my opinion it is. The reason lies in the patient's extensive use of avoidance defenses.

The reader will recall the patient described in Chapter 4, a young social scientist who was progressing well professionally. Mr. A.'s specialty allowed him to remain relatively distant from people, but his inability to form stable relationships and his sense of aloneness and hopelessness had brought him to the brink of suicide. He entered psychotherapy and very quickly became deeply involved in borderline issues. The belief that he would be, and the feeling that indeed he was, abandoned by his therapist dominated the work of the first year. At the same time he gradually and intermittently became aware of intense longing for the therapist. As treatment proceeded he recognized vague sexual feelings toward the therapist that resembled those that he had felt as a child when he stood close to his mother, pressing his head into her abdomen. He also became aware of urges to rush or fall into his therapist's chest; he was afraid because he felt that he might, in fact, destroy his therapist in this way, or perhaps be destroyed himself.

With these transference developments, he resumed an old practice of promiscuous, casual homosexual activities. He reported seeking to perform fellatio when he was under pressure of severe yearning to be with the therapist. In one treatment hour he described these feelings and activities as he had experienced them the night before. and then he added a new self-observation. Looking away to one side, he quietly, almost under his breath, said he had found himself "sucking like a baby." Generalized obfuscation followed this admission. Everything he said was vague, rambling, and indefinite. The therapist hoped that this new information could be kept conscious and available to awareness. It would be important for later interpretation of the infant-to-mother transference: that the patient was experiencing the same urgent need for sustenance from the therapist that he had continued since infancy to experience in relation to his mother—a need to suck milk from the breast-penis.

Later in the hour he returned to his experience the night before. Once again his narration became clear as he described his longing for the therapist and search for homosexual contact, but he omitted any mention of his infantile feelings and sucking activity. The therapist suspected that the patient had mobilized some method of avoiding, perhaps denial, or at least of withholding. In an attempt to counter this defense, the therapist made a confrontation. When the patient seemed to have finished retelling the story, the therapist directly, with emphasis and with minimal inflection, said, "And you found yourself sucking like a baby." The patient winced, turned his face away, and was briefly silent. Then he said, "Yes, I know." In another short silence he turned his head back toward the therapist; then he continued his associations. He did not directly pursue the matter that had been forced to his attention, but it was clear that he had fully acknowledged it and was aware that his therapist also knew about it. Because of the patient's fear of feeling close to the therapist, the therapist chose not to confront any further. He felt that any further attempt to hold the patient to the subject in that session would now be more threatening than constructive.

## CONFRONTATION THAT IS URGENTLY REQUIRED

Work with borderline patients can be quite different from that just described. By contrast, some hours are characterized by intense involvement in one, several, or all aspects of life at the borderline level. Help may be urgently needed at these times to deal with two multiply determined problems: (1) the patient's becoming overwhelmed with the belief and feeling that he is in danger and (2) his taking unwitting action through which he puts himself in real danger. At these times he needs help to recognize (1) the actual safety afforded by reality, especially the reality of his relationship with the therapist, and (2) the actual danger involved in using certain pathological relationships, in taking action on fear and instinctual drive pressures, and in failing to acknowledge that what he fears arises only from within himself. Ordinarily one would expect a patient to accept reassuring, reality-oriented help of this kind. Paradoxically, the borderline patient may resist it, even fight it, mobilizing avoidance for that purpose. Then confrontation is required. Let us now consider this situation in detail.

The borderline patient's feeling of being in serious danger no matter which way he turns is of utmost importance. One leading determinant of this fear is his belief that he will be or is abandoned. Another is his impulses, which he feels threaten destruction of the objects he depends on. This threat in turn means being alone or being destroyed. Self-esteem at these times is demolished; his primitive superego threatens corporal or capital punishment. Simultaneously reality gains little recognition and holds little sway.

When overwhelmed or about to be overwhelmed with this complex experience, the patient needs the support of reality. Of course, I do not advocate empty reassurance. If his controls are so tenuous that a threatening situation really exists, steps in management are required to provide safety. For example, hospitalization may be indicated. In most cases, however, what the patient needs most of all is the real reassurance that he will not be abandoned and that no one will be destroyed. If the therapist tries to respond to this need with simply clarifying or reality testing, he often meets resistance. The patient avoids acknowledging the safety provided by reality, especially the reality of his relationship with his therapist. Confrontation is needed to meet this avoidance.

Why does the patient sometimes avoid acknowledging the safety afforded by reality—for example, that his relationship with this therapist is secure? There are three reasons: (1) The fear of being abandoned (and destroyed) arises, for most borderline patients, out of real experiences over prolonged periods of time with primary objects. Through certain complex mechanisms this experience has been perpetuated throughout their lives in subsequent relationships that they have formed in the quest for sustenance. A large part of their experience, then, speaks against the therapist's version of reality. The patient fears to risk accepting the therapist's offer as if the therapist were leading him to destruction. (2) The force of the patient's raging hunger and his partial fixation at the level of magical thinking convince him that he really is a danger to people he cares about and needs. Even though he may acknowledge them to be of no danger to him, he fears using relationships when he so vividly believes that he will destroy his objects. (3) These patients use projection to avoid the recognition that the supposedly dangerous, raging hunger arises within themselves. The patient's acknowledgment that his object is safe, rather than dangerous, threatens the breakdown of this defense. These three fears may be experienced unconsciously or may be preconscious, conscious but denied, or even conscious and acknowledged.

Now let us turn to the problem of the borderline patient's putting himself in actual danger. Of course, danger in his life can spring from many sources. But the one germane to discussion of confrontation is his use of avoidance mechanisms, so that he remains insufficiently aware of the dangers as he acts. Specifically he employs avoidances against recognizing (1) the real danger in certain relationships, (2) the real danger in action used as a defense mechanism, and (3) the real danger in action used for discharge of impulses and feelings.

The potentially dangerous relationships are those he forms with other borderline or psychotic persons, persons who seek primarily after exclusive possession and succor. They are also ridden with fears and destructive urges upon which they tend to act. The patient may throw himself into togetherness with such borderline or psychotic persons, believing he has found a wonderful mutual closeness and perhaps feeling saved and exhilarated. In fact, the reality basis for the relationship is tenuous, if present at all. It simply provides the illusion, partially gained vicariously, of gratifying each other's needs for infantile closeness. Belief in the goodness and security of the partner may be maintained through the mechanism of splitting. Denial and distortion also may serve to obfuscate the partner's real ambivalence, instability, and untrustworthiness. Inevitably the partner will act destructively, independently, or in concert with the patient's own destructiveness. The least noxious outcome is desertion by one or the other. In any event, with their high hopes they ride for a fall, one that precipitates the full borderline conflict, often in crisis proportions. The therapist must realize the risk in these relationships and try to show it to the patient; otherwise he

must at least set limits. Often the patient will not acknowledge the reality that his therapist tries to bring to his
attention and will not heed the limits set down. The lure of
infant–mother closeness is too great. Furthermore, acting
upon it with the friend may relieve by displacement his
similar urges toward his therapist. But most important,
acknowledging the real danger in such a relationship would
mean giving it up and experiencing an abandonment following closely on the heels of wonderful hope. So the patient
avoids the reality, and the therapist must return to confrontation.

Borderline patients are inclined to endanger themselves
by resorting to action as a defensive measure. For example,
if psychological avoidances become insufficient, the patient
may take refuge in literal flight—perhaps run out of the
therapist's office, fail to keep appointments, or travel to
some distant place. If in the process he deprives himself of
needed support from the therapist, he may be unable to
check his frightening fantasies and impulses. Decompensation or other forms of harm may result. Another means of
defensive flight is offered in drugs and alcohol; the dangers
are obvious to the therapist. Some patients use displacement
in order to allow their destructive impulses toward the
therapist to be expressed in action. While avoiding acknowledgment of rage at the therapist, the patient can be unleash-
ing it on the outside world. He may break windows, verbally
attack policemen, or incite brawls, meanwhile mobilizing
various rationalizations to justify his behavior. All the while
he keeps out of awareness his bristling hostility toward his
therapist.

The borderline patient may also use endangering action
simply as a means of discharging a variety of highly pressing impulses. Through harmful activities, including self-

destruction, he can express all his various sources of destructive urges and his wishes to incorporate and merge. Drugs, alcohol, promiscuity, suicide to gain Nirvana, pregnancy, and obesity form a partial list of these harmful activities. The patient resists giving up both the destructive and the incorporative activities. To do so would mean bearing the pressure of unrelieved impulses.

In all these instances of using action in the service of defense or impulse discharge, the patient to some degree avoids recognizing that his actions are, in fact, dangerous to himself. If he knows this danger intellectually, he is likely to say that he has no feeling about it, that it does not seem real, or that it does not matter. This avoidance allows him to pursue the endangering activity unchecked. Mere reality testing and limit setting will not induce him to recognize that he endangers himself and must work to give the activity up. By combining confrontation with reality testing and limit setting, however, the therapist can often break through the denial and accomplish this aim.

There remains one more danger in the use of avoidance mechanisms, one that was mentioned in an earlier section. This danger involves massive denial of intense feelings and impulses. It is true that much of the time there is no need to force a patient to face denied feelings and impulses, but there are occasions when it is urgently necessary to do so. For example, the patient may be under the extreme pressure of wanting to kill his therapist and, as a defensive alternative, may be on the verge of actually killing himself. In order not to be aware of such unbearable emotional and impulsive pressures, the patient is capable of massive use of denial and other avoidance devices. He may avoid to the point of literally eclipsing all feelings from his subjective view. Distressing as it is for him to face what he is avoiding, the nonhospitalized patient cannot be allowed this much denial; it is too dangerous. It is dangerous because totally denied intense impulses and feelings are especially subject to expression in uncontrollable, destructive action. This action may take place with a sudden burst of feelings, or it may occur in a robotlike state of nonfeeling. Clarification and reality testing are to no avail against massive denial. Confrontation is required. The therapist's aims are (1) to help the patient become aware of his impulses, so that he need not be subject to action without warning; (2) to help him gain temporary relief through abreaction; and (3) to help him gain a rational position from which he can exert self-control or seek help in maintaining control. At this point it is essential to provide the patient with sustaining support sufficient to enable him to bear the otherwise unbearable. It may not be possible to support adequately with the therapist–patient relationship alone; temporary hospitalization may be needed as an adjunct.

All facets of the urgent need for confrontation cannot be illustrated in a single clinical example, but two are involved in the vignette that follows. One involves the patient's being overwhelmed with the belief that he is in danger of abandonment; the other relates to his putting himself in danger by discharging feelings through action. The episode to be discussed took place a few weeks after the last reported session in the treatment of Mr. A.

It had become clear that Mr. A. used considerable repression and that he also depended heavily on avoidance devices, especially denial. But these devices were not enough to meet his needs for defense; he also consciously withheld thoughts and affects, was vague, and usually avoided looking at the therapist. Details of a traumatic childhood had emerged. For periods of up to a year he had been abandoned by his mother and left to the care of a childless and

emotionally distant aunt and uncle. His mother had fluc-
tuated widely in her attitude toward him, at times intensely
close in a bodily seductive way, at other times uncaring or
coldly hostile. She and his father made a practice of sneaking
off for evenings after he had fallen asleep. To ensure that he
would remain in the house, they removed the door knobs
and took them with them. Repeatedly he awoke and found
himself alone, trapped, and panicky for prolonged periods.

To summarize the earlier description, the most prominent quality of his transference was the belief that his
therapist did not think about him or care about him. Outside
the treatment hours, the patient frequently felt that the
therapist did not exist. He suffered marked aloneness, yearning, and rage, increasingly centered around the person of
the therapist. The therapist's work had primarily involved
clarifying the emerging transference and relating it to early
experiences and life patterns. The therapist also repeatedly
implied that he, the therapist, was not like the patient's
mother and not like the patient felt him to be; rather, he
was solidly caring and trustworthy. The patient's feelings,
however, intensified, and he began to seek relief by occasionally discharging them through action. It was at this time
that he increased his homosexual activities, and the previously reported hour occurred. At the same time more rage
was emerging. Many times the therapist interpreted that
the patient's impulses and rage were so intense because he
believed he was really alone, uncared for, and absent from
the therapist's thoughts. Each time the reality of the relationship was also implied. But the patient seemed unable to
accept it.

Before long the patient put himself in serious danger.
Rage with the supposedly abandoning therapist dominated
him. He got drunk, purposely drove recklessly across a
bridge, and smashed his car on the guard rail. Although he

himself showed little concern for his safety, he was concerned about how the therapist would react. Would the therapist be uncaring, as he expected?

Clarification, interpretation, and indication of the reality of the relationship had not been effective before. They would be less effective now. Certainly merely pointing out the danger of his action would make little impression. The therapist elected to include confrontation in his efforts. First he repeated the interpretation: that the patient's erroneous belief that the therapist did not exist was the source of his intense anger. Next the therapist confronted the patient with the actual danger he had put himself in by discharging his rage in action. With emphatic concern the therapist said, "You could have been hurt, even killed! It was very dangerous for you to do that, and it is very important that it not happen again." Now the patient tacitly acknowledged the danger. Confrontation had succeeded. It was followed by a second confrontation, one designed to gain the patient's acknowledgment that the therapist really cared about him. The therapist said:

> The way to avoid this danger is to work with your feeling and belief that I do not care or do not exist. By all means, whenever you approach believing it, whenever you begin to feel the intense rage which naturally follows, call me up. Call me, talk with me, and in that way find out that I really do exist, that I am not gone.

Superficially this maneuver would seem to have been a manipulation, but in fact it was a confrontation, presented very concretely. Its message was that the therapist was in reality a reliable, caring person whom it was safe to trust. The patient responded with what seemed to be a half-hearted acknowledgment and agreement. But he did not again endanger himself in any similar way.

About three weeks later, however, he experienced the same very intense transference feelings and impulses. He drank heavily and made contact with a group of homosexuals who were strangers to him. He went with them to a loft in a slum section of the city and awoke there the next morning. He found himself alone, nude, and unaware of what had happened. He was frightened at the time, but not when he told his therapist about it. The therapist responded by first showing his feelings of strong concern as he agreed that it had been a dangerous experience. He thus presented what amounted to a confrontation against rather weak denial of danger and fright. Then he clarified the psychodynamic pattern along the lines already described; he showed the patient that he had put himself in danger by taking action to express his yearnings for, and rage with, his frustrating, supposedly uncaring, therapist. Next came a combination of limit setting and confrontation:

This behavior is much too dangerous, and you must not allow yourself to take such risks again. You felt so intensely because you believed I did not care. Anytime you feel this way and are in danger of acting on it, contact me instead. It would be much better, much safer, to talk with me on the phone. Please do so, whenever it is necessary, at any time of day or night. See that I exist and that this relationship is real.

The patient gave the impression of neither agreeing nor disagreeing. He never called. But there were no recurrences of discharging intense feelings and impulses in any dangerous actions. Two months later the patient was overwhelmed with fears of closeness with the therapist, and he felt suicidal. But he took no action; instead, he requested a brief hospitalization. He was discharged at his own request after five days.

# Eight

# Misuses of Confrontation

Although convinced of the importance of confrontation in treating borderline patients, I have also been impressed with the vulnerability of such patients to the misuses of confrontation. Misuse of confrontation can arise from faulty clinical understanding as well as from the therapist's transference and countertransference problems. In this chapter I shall discuss the misuse of confrontation and in the process begin to shift the focus of my considerations away from the patient to the therapist and his countertransference difficulties in borderline psychotherapy.

## The Borderline Patient's Vulnerability to Harm from Confrontation

Because of his intense impulses and inadequate defenses, the borderline patient's psychic equilibrium is tenuous. For him, confrontation is a powerful instrument that can be as harmful as it can be helpful. Confrontation is most useful in a setting that takes into account the tenuous working relationship with most borderline patients. A good working relationship requires that the patient be able to trust in the therapist's judgment and constructive purpose. I am referring here not only to basic trust, but also to a trust gained through experience that the therapist will not harm the patient by placing him under more stress than he can tolerate and use. Because the trust is tenuous for a long time with these patients, the therapist, in using confrontation, must observe certain restrictions and precautions in order not to undermine that trust. I shall list and discuss these restrictions and precautions, not as a set of rules, but as matters to take into account when deciding how, when, and about what to confront.

*Assess Reality Stress in the Patient's Current Life.* When a patient is under serious stress in his life—for instance, when a loss is impending—we do not want to load him with even more stress in therapy. Clinical judgment regarding the amount of stress a patient is bearing is often difficult; it requires thoughtfulness, empathy, and an examination of mental status. This task is particularly difficult with patients who can employ avoidance devices as defenses. The patient can be near a breaking point and yet feel and show little evidence of it. Only with the additional aid of thoughtful appraisal of the patient's real-life situation and psychological makeup can the therapist reliably evaluate how much stress the patient is experiencing and how much more he can stand. The therapist can then decide whether a confrontation should be made at that time and, if it should, how much support is needed along with it.

*Avoid Breaking Down Needed Defenses.* This precaution applies with all types of patients. With borderline personalities, however, these defenses, especially denial, are brittle. Although they may at times be massive and formidable, they are inclined to give way to confrontation all at once. The patient may be overwhelmed with impulses and fears as well as with a sense of worthlessness and badness. All sorts of confrontations can have this effect— not only those aiming at awareness of impulses but also those promoting acknowledgment of the therapist's caring for and valuing the patient.

*Avoid Overstimulating the Patient's Wish for Closeness.* In the feelings and beliefs of these patients, closeness always carries with it the threat of destroying and being destroyed. Showing strong feelings of any type can stimulate the wish for or feeling of closeness. So can being personal in any way—for instance, telling a personal anecdote. At certain times these patients can be overstimulated quite easily. Even the therapist's leaning forward in his chair for emphasis can be too much. Heightened oral-level urges, fear, and defensive rage can ensue, flight or some form of endangering action may result, and the tenuous working relationship may be lost in the course of the rage. In his anger the patient may feel that he has destroyed the therapist within himself or that he has evicted the therapist from the premises of his person. In this way his rage sets up a chain reaction. He is now alone within, and the intense borderline experience is precipitated: fear of abandonment and aloneness, raging destructive oral urges to get the therapist back inside again, panic over the destructiveness and expected retaliation, and efforts to protect himself by rejecting the therapist further, thus only increasing his aloneness.

*Avoid Overstimulating the Patient's Rage.* Confrontation may involve deprivation and frustration for the patient. It may also involve a show of anger by the therapist. In either case, these patients, who much of the time labor under considerable pressure of denied and suppressed anger, are easily stimulated to overburdening levels of rage. Usually the patient's rage also brings fear, panic, and ultimately a sense of annihilation. The ensuing dangers are the same as those evoked by overstimulation with closeness.

*Avoid Confrontation of Narcissistic Entitlement.* As long as a patient is in a borderline state, he feels and believes that his subjective being is threatened—his entitlement to survive, as it were. I have already suggested the ways in which this entitlement to survive can be distinguished from narcissistic entitlement, and yet one can easily be mistaken for the other. Some therapists believe they must help borderline patients to modify their narcissistic entitlement. It is important that these therapists not misdiagnose entitlement to survive as narcissistic entitlement. If they make this mistake, they will believe they are confronting therapeutically a wish to which the patient feels entitled, when actually they are threatening him with harm by attacking a fundamental need: his entitlement to survive.

In my opinion, direct work with narcissistic entitlement should not be undertaken at all until adequately functioning holding introjects are firmly enough established to prevent regression into aloneness and significant loss of self-cohesiveness. My experience indicates that as long as entitlement to survive is insecure, narcissistic entitlement is needed as a source of some feeling of self-worth, power, and security, even though it is at the level of infantile omnipotence and liable to give way transiently to its obverse. Indeed, the patient's narcissistic entitlement may be a significant force in keeping him alive. The confrontation of narcissistic entitlement can demolish self-esteem and security and leave the patient feeling worthless, helpless, and evil for having made inappropriate demands. He is then more vulnerable to threats to his entitlement to survive, such as aloneness and helplessness against annihilatory dangers. The patient will react with rage to this exposure to danger. If he is strong enough, his rage can lead to redoubled insistence on his narcissistic entitlement, along with some degree of protective withdrawal. If he does not have the strength to reassert his narcissistic entitlement, he will probably in his rage have to reject and in fantasy destroy the therapist, or become seriously suicidal. Desperate aloneness must be the result; with it comes the panic of being overwhelmed, and the rest of the borderline conflict follows.

## Countertransference Issues that Lead to the Misuse of Confrontation

Within the intense dyadic relationship that these patients form with the therapist, they can experience with great urgency the issues of annihilation and aloneness already discussed. The patient yearns to be held, fed, and touched and often becomes angry and despairing when his infantile demands are not gratified. The therapist, in response, may feel that the patient literally has to be rescued and may therefore tend to give the patient more and more time, support, and reassurance. This dangerous kind of giving by the therapist may satisfy some patients and alleviate the emptiness and despair for short, or even longer, periods of time. At best it offers a corrective emotional experience for the deprivations of the patient's earlier life. But more often than not, this giving with the feeling of having to rescue the patient opens the door to further regressive wishes and angry demands. For this type of patient, nothing is enough, and the therapist's nurturant response may lead to further regression. Balint (1968) describes this phenomenon in therapy as a "malignant regression." The therapist, facing persistent demands in spite of the great deal he has already given, may feel helpless and depleted and may become increasingly angry that this giving does so little good—indeed, it seems to make the patient emptier and more desperate. The therapist may also feel envious of the patient's demandingness itself and his apparent success in arousing intense rescuing responses in other persons. At such a point a therapist may use confrontation as a vehicle for expressing his fury and envy. Rather than a confrontation with which the therapist attempts empathically to put the patient in touch with something he is avoiding, it may be an assault on the patient's narcissistic entitlement—in reality a hostile manipulation. For example, the therapist may angrily state that the patient has to give up these outrageous, infantile demands. As described earlier, asking the patient to give up narcissistic demands at a time when he is struggling with an entitlement to survive can be disastrous for the patient, whether or not the regression to the life-and-death position was provoked by the therapist's initial rescuing response. In addition, because these patients have a primitive, severely punitive superego that they easily project onto others and reintroject, the therapist's anger as he attacks is readily confused by the patient with his own and may strengthen the destructive self-punishing position that the patient has already established.

Even when the therapist does not respond to the patient by acting on wishes to rescue him, the patient will often feel increasing anger during treatment. He expects nurturance from the therapist and envies all that the therapist possesses. At times this anger is provoked by something that makes the therapist less accessible—an illness or preoccupation with a personal issue—and may take the form of a devaluing, sadistic assault on the therapist. The patient may minimize the importance of the therapist in his life, destroy anything the therapist attempts to give, or devalue whatever the therapist says as incorrect, inadequate, or inconsequential (for further comments on devaluation, see Chapter 10). For the therapist this attack can be a painful, dehumanizing experience in which he feels isolated, helpless, and totally unimportant to another human being, especially if he has had little experience with these patients and does not recognize the attack as part of the transference. Because all therapists wish to be helpful and competent, such behavior by the patient can be particularly distressing. In this setting a supposed confrontation by the therapist may, in fact, serve as an attack in defense against his feelings of intense isolation and abandonment by his patient. It may also be retaliatory. What the therapist overlooks in his distress is that what he is experiencing so intensely at the hands of his patient is what the patient feels at the roots of psychopathology and has usually experienced repeatedly and severely early in his life. Such oversight by the therapist means loss of potential therapeutic work.

I would like to illustrate these points with reference to the treatment of a borderline patient, Ms. E., "confronted" about her narcissism at a time when she was concerned with her ability to survive. Ms. E. was a 23-year-old, single secretary who had been hospitalized following the termination of four years of psychotherapy. She had felt her therapist to be aloof, ungiving, and uninterested personally in her. Although the therapy ended by mutual agreement, the patient began to feel increasingly abandoned, empty, desperate, and suicidal. During her hospitalization the tenuous life-and-death quality of her life was spelled out; it included a long history of abandonment by important people and her inability to tolerate her fury and disappointment when this abandonment occurred. While in the hospital she began therapy with a new psychiatrist whom she felt was empathically in tune with her. Although there were many tense moments for the patient, therapist, and hospital staff, she gradually became more comfortable and was able to leave the hospital to return to her job. Shortly after her release, her therapist had an accident in which he sustained a serious comminuted fracture of his leg. Not only did he suddenly miss several sessions with the patient but he felt less emotionally available, more preoccupied with himself, and unable to talk about the accident with his patient. He also experienced a sense of personal vulnerability. The patient began to complain angrily about his not caring enough and about his lack of understanding her feelings. The obvious vulnerability of her therapist to these devaluing attacks led the patient to talk increasingly about her love and admiration for him, while she covertly nursed her fury and concern for his vulnerability. The therapist later acknowledged that he found the patient's love gratifying and relieving.

Gradually, however, the patient became increasingly suicidal and required readmission to the hospital. During her sessions with the therapist in the hospital, her angry complaints reappeared with increasing demands that he be more available, give her more, and stop using her treatment for personal gratification for himself. She also acknowledged how concerned she was for her therapist's physical condition and how important he was to her. The therapist's continued inability to respond adequately to this acknowledgment led to further complaints. His own fury grew. After several more sessions of these complaints, he responded angrily, asking the patient why she considered herself so special, why she felt entitled to so much—more than he gave any other patient. The patient then became more frightened and increasingly suicidal.

Following this session the therapist obtained a consultation in which he spelled out his feelings of vulnerability since his accident, his discomfort about it when the patient brought it up, his relative emotional unavailability, and his discomfort with the patient's demands and attacks. He felt that his preoccupation with his injury had made him feel helpless, passive, and less resilient in the face of the patient's concerns and angry attacks. Now he saw his angry statement as a retaliatory gesture to counter his helpless rage during the patient's assaults. He was able to go back to the patient and help her to explore her feelings about his accident; he could also tell her some of the details about it. Both the patient and therapist felt relief, and the patient could speak angrily about her disappointment in her therapist for not being omnipotent, her concern that he was vulnerable, her belief that she had magically harmed him, and her fear of expressing her fury toward him once she felt he could not take it. After these sessions the patient was able to return to her previous and more integrated level of functioning.

I want to stress here the sense of helplessness experienced by the therapist in the face of a patient who seems unresponsive to his efforts. The patient's unyielding passivity may arouse a defensive activity in the therapist, who tries increasingly to clarify or interpret away the patient's regressive position. Balint (1968) and Little (1960, 1966) emphasize the importance of the reliving and working through of this position in the treatment of such patients and describe the difficulties that arise when the therapist feels that he has to make the regression disappear. In order to help the patient work through the regression, the therapist must come face to face with prolonged, unbearable feelings of depression, emptiness, despair, loneliness, fury, and a sense of annihilation, both in the patient and in himself. For long stretches empathic listening with clarifying questions may be the only activity required of the therapist. But as time passes, the burden the therapist has to shoulder may become overwhelming. He may then choose the angry, attacking, pseudoconfrontation as a means of seeking relief: He expresses a demand to the patient to give up such behavior.

There are basically three types of countertransference difficulties that may occur in the treatment of the borderline patient and that are relevant to the issue of confrontation: (1) the therapist's wish to maintain the gratifying position of nurturant mother, (2) the therapist's response to the biting attacks of the patient, and (3) the therapist's wish to have a well-behaved patient.

Although the wishes of these patients to be one with their therapist can frighten both patient and therapist, there are also gratifying aspects to such longings. The omnipotence that the patient ascribes to the therapist as he (the patient) recreates the mother–infant dyadic tie can give the therapist much pleasure. In fact, the therapist may wish this tie to remain forever, in spite of his commitment to help the patient grow up. As the patient works through the infantile regression and as more mature choices become open to him, he may begin to take steps away from the therapist-mother. At this point a bereft therapist may repeatedly "confront" the patient with the lack of wisdom of the choice or with the therapist's feeling that they have not sufficiently explored the step the patient wants to take. At the same time, the therapist ignores the patient's healthy side and its growth in therapy. Consciously, the therapist sees himself as being helpful and cautious, but in effect he is manipulating to maintain the gratification of the infantile tie with the patient. The result is a patient stuck in this dyadic tie to his therapist because of countertransference wishes of the therapist. The therapist has used pseudoconfrontation, manipulation, or suggestion to keep the patient from growing up.

Because these patients' wishes for nurturance cannot be totally gratified by the therapist, the patient ultimately has to shift from warm sucking to angry biting in his relationship to the therapist. The patient's rage may destroy the sense of gratification the therapist was receiving from the previous, positive relationship with the patient. Rather than accept the rage as a crucial part of the treatment (Winnicott 1969), the therapist may repeatedly "confront" the patient with accusations that he is running from his positive feelings for the therapist. In the specific situation I am describing such confrontation is not useful. Again, it is instead a manipulation or pseudoconfrontation that serves primarily as a defense for the therapist against his discomfort with the patient's fury, and as a means to maintain the gratification of the positive dyadic tie with the patient. These manipulations also make a demand upon the patient. When they are about the patient's entitlement, they tell the patient that, if he chooses to retain a piece of behavior, he is bad and out of the therapist's favor.

The issue of the patient's "badness" is important in the treatment of borderline patients. Many of these patients present with their neurotic defenses and adaptive capacities more in evidence. The stress of some outside traumatic event or the intensity of the psychotherapeutic situation itself, however, is usually sufficient to lead to regressive use of borderline defenses and the emergence of primitive wishes, demands, and fears. The therapist may feel that there is a deliberate, manipulative quality to this regression and thus view the patient as bad. This response occurs most intensely in therapists who are inexperienced in working with borderline patients or in those who are frightened by their patient's regressive manifestations (Frosch 1967). As a countertransference response, the therapist may use an angry pseudoconfrontation to punish the "bad" patient and to get him to give up his bad behavior or face losing the therapist's love and approval. Needless to say, this position is extremely threatening to the borderline patient, who has blurred ego and superego boundaries, a primitive superego, and fears of abandonment, engulfment, and annihilation. It intensifies feelings that his own sense of worthlessness and badness is indeed correct.

Even the experienced therapist usually feels some anger in working with regressed borderline patients. Is it possible for him, when necessary, to use his anger in constructive, forceful, appropriate confrontations? I think it is, so long as he has no wish to destroy the patient—not even his sick side. I recognize that this attitude is an ideal; in practice the therapist inevitably has some destructive wishes and must be consciously in touch with them if he is to avoid putting them into action. If no harm is to come from angry confrontation, these destructive wishes need to be balanced by the therapist's desire to be helpful to his patient and by his struggle to master his own destructiveness. The therapist's capacity to stay in empathic touch with his patient enables him to monitor the amount of force he can use without having the patient subjectively experience the force as an attack. Thus the therapist's awareness both of the character structure of the patient, with its vulnerabilities, and of his own sadistic, destructive urges places him in a position to use confrontation constructively, even when angry.

Many borderline patients do not easily learn that the therapist can be trusted and relied on. For them, the frightening experiences of their rage and the projection of it onto the world may result in perpetual distrust and isolation, no matter how trustworthy the therapist is, behaves, or states he is to the patient. I feel that the experiencing of murderous rage in the transference and nonretaliation by the therapist are crucial for many of these patients. Only then can the transference experience occur that ultimately removes the terror or aggression and the frightening primitive ways of getting rid of it. When the patient observes his therapist struggling successfully with his own countertransference fury, he has the opportunity to learn how another person can master murderous rage and to internalize important new ways of tolerating fury and using its derivatives constructively. If the therapist fails in his struggle, the patient may then comply helplessly as the victim of an attack and thus reconfirm his view of the world as untrustworthy. Through his observations of the therapist's struggle, the patient can learn most effectively that neither he nor the therapist, in spite of mutually destructive urges, need destroy the other.

# Nine

# Regression in Psychotherapy
## Disruptive or Therapeutic?

Discussions about the usefulness of regressions in psychotherapy often arouse feelings that can polarize the participants. Interpretation of the transference in psychotherapy is viewed by some as inducing regression and therefore dangerous, and by others as a helpful tool that may limit regression, especially as the negative transference emerges.

How can we explain the contradictions, heat, and confusion in an aspect of psychotherapy that is manifest so frequently in therapists' work with patients? I believe that among the factors involved is a lack of clarity with regard to certain crucial questions: (1) What do we mean by a regression in psychotherapy? Is it a return to early unresolved or safe modes of functioning that is part of an experience within the psychotherapeutic situation that both patient and therapist can observe? Or is it a disintegrative

experience that disrupts therapy and the patient's and sometimes the therapist's life? Or is it sometimes a combination
or alternation of both? (2) When a regression occurs in
psychotherapy, does the therapist believe that a specific
regression, or regressions in general, are destructive to the
psychotherapeutic goals and should therefore be discouraged
or viewed with concern? Or does the therapist feel that a
regression can sometimes offer "a new beginning" (Balint
1968) or an opportunity to resolve earlier conflicts? And
how can he decide whether one regression is destructive
while another is therapeutic? (3) Does the personality of the
therapist permit comfort with the specific area of the
patient's regression, or does he use defenses that change the
character of the regression and its utility to the patient?
(4) Is the patient's diagnosis important in determining the
usefulness of a regression? Is a regression in a neurotic
patient more desirable than a regression in a borderline
patient, and under what circumstances?

Implicit in the regression than can occur in the psycho-
analysis of a neurotic patient is a feeling, usually shared by
both patient and analyst, of a sense of basic safety. The
regression has a slow evolution and unfolding and usually is
preceded by the establishment of the positive transference
aspects of a therapeutic alliance. Within it the patient
maintains a capacity to observe himself, has the ability to
delay acting on any impulses and wishes that may emerge,
reserving them for an affective reliving within the analytic
hour, and can make use of the analyst's clarifications and
interpretations in integrating the regressive experience. At
its best, a transference neurosis develops, that is, the analytic
situation and the analyst become a major concern of the
patient; within the analysis the patient relives a previously
unresolved conflictual area, with the analyst representing
the early important objects, previously internalized but

now projected onto the analyst. At the same time, the patient can make the distinction between the analyst as a real person and the wishes, feelings, and conflicts he places on the analyst that belong to the past. Although many of his thoughts and fantasies are involved in his analysis, the rest of the patient's life does not become enmeshed with the analytic regression; as a result, the emerging conflicts do not get acted out in the patient's daily life. This ideal, though rarely attained, picture of a therapeutic alliance and transference neurosis partially explains the basic comfort of the patient and the analyst; in spite of fantasies to the contrary, there is often little that is significantly disruptive or uncontrolled. And the acting out that is most invariably present is usually nondestructive, although it may impede the analytic process. The regression is clearly "in the service of the ego" (Kris 1952); the reliving of old, unresolved childhood conflicts offers the adult in the analytic situation the opportunity to find new and more adaptive solutions.

In contrast, patients with borderline personality organization can present a very different picture of regression in a psychotherapeutic or psychoanalytic situation. Because the life-and-death, devour-or-be-devoured issues are not settled in these patients, and their ego structure lacks the flexibility and synthetic capacity to allow gradual regressive movement and to modulate the intensity of affects, the regression can be a disruptive, all-or-nothing, frightening experience, either transiently or over a long period. In addition, these patients, especially during a regression, have difficulty separating inner from outer, and use primitive defenses such as splitting, projection, projective identification, and primitive idealization (Kernberg 1967) or go through long periods of fusion with the therapist (Little 1960). Understandably, such events do not allow a clear distinction between patient and therapist, and leave blurred what belongs to the patient's past and present, and what is projected onto the therapist or is really the therapist. In such a world, where relationships are experienced as full of danger to the patient, trust and a capacity to observe, listen, and integrate can be absent or only transiently present. The dyadic psychotherapeutic relationship can be the stressful stimulus that triggers unresolved feelings of abandonment and neglect, and the emergence of early childhood needs followed by rage, since these needs cannot be fulfilled in any adult relationship. The ensuing regression can be a furious, destructive clinging in which the desperation of the patient increases as he destroys the memories of good sustaining introjects, including those of his therapist. He also develops the feeling that he no longer has any relationship or contact with the real therapist. With the sense of loss of a sustaining relationship with the therapist, the regressive feelings and behavior can easily extend outside the therapy hours with the possibility of serious acting out, including suicide. Another aspect of the regression can be the emergence of a desperate, helpless withdrawal and isolation, which Guntrip (1971) feels is at the core of the difficulty in this group of patients, and which can be very difficult for patient and therapist to bear.

Because regressions in psychotherapy of other than "ideal, analyzable patients" may have a disruptive and even life-endangering potential, may bring frightening material into the therapy, and may possibly seriously affect the patient's daily functioning, why not do everything possible to prevent regressions in those patients whose regression does not seem to have clear features of a controlled, analyzable transference, or transference neurosis? Alternately, can we at least define as clearly as possible when this painful and potentially dangerous regression is useful, or especially important? Studies by workers who have had significant experience with patients who have a serious regressive potential, such as Balint (1968), Guntrip (1971), Little (1960, 1966), Rosenfeld (1965), and Winnicott (1965), suggest that regression in borderline, schizoid, or schizophrenic patients offers the possibility for a "new beginning" or a "rebirth." These workers firmly believe that regression in psychotherapy has the possibility of exposing the basic vulnerability that resulted from very early and usually repeated experiences involving an environment that did not respond adequately to the needs of the infant and very small child. The regression permits a reliving that can lead to a partial repair of an old wound. Little (1960), in particular, writes about "basic unity," a return to the undifferentiated state of earliest infancy as a painful but sometimes necessary regression that ultimately permits a new differentiation and integration.

My own experiences, although of much shorter duration than these workers', convince me of the validity of their position. I am referring to the usefulness of therapeutic regression in a group of patients in the borderline spectrum who might function adequately in certain areas and who can even make gains in the kind of psychotherapy that discourages regression but whose lives have a quality of conformity and a sense of unreality described in the literature as a "false self" (Winnicott 1960). The "false selves" of these patients—the price they pay in order to function adequately—may not permit satisfying mutual relationships to the extent that they protect patients from their underlying wishes and fears. It is much easier to modify symptoms than to affect profoundly a person's way of feeling and caring about himself and others.

It is also important to keep separate from the patients I am discussing the majority of patients who come to a therapist for help: people who have an essentially solid sense of themselves and who can benefit from brief or longer therapy that does not have to include any significant regressive component. And, as I have stated, patients in the borderline group can benefit significantly from therapy that carefully steers clear of regression, especially when therapeutic goals can be reached without it and without the potential dangers that accompany it.

I think that most therapists, even if they believe in the possible usefulness of regression in this group of patients, do not begin psychotherapy with a new patient with the idea that they will encourage a regression. Most of them are all too aware of the possible turmoil and potential self-destructiveness that could be unleashed. They would probably agree that a careful diagnostic assessment, possibly requiring many sessions, is crucial. The task includes acquiring some understanding of the patient's problems, conflicts, strengths, and weaknesses, a feeling for how solid a sense of self he has, and the formulation of a treatment plan. Important in the assessment is the use the patient makes of the therapist, assuming a "good-enough" therapist. Among the questions are: Does the patient develop a relationship with the therapist over time that demonstrates increasing trust and a sense that he and the therapist are whole people? Can the patient make use of the therapist and the therapist's comments as a sustaining force as well as a person who helps him to "acknowledge, bear, and put in perspective" (Semrad 1969) significant aspects of his life, or does he have to reject and devalue the therapist from the beginning? Can the patient make use of a careful, supportive look at recent stressful events that may have precipitated his current difficulties? Can he work with the therapist to recognize difficulties in his relationships with important people and make use of his understanding within these relationships? Can he see the role guilt has played in his life story and relate it to difficulties with present relationships? Does the patient make use of the sessions to confirm his own sense of badness, or to find constructive understanding and alternatives? The answers to these and other diagnostic questions determine the level on which therapy has to proceed as the therapist formulates his understanding of the patient's difficulties and capacities in order to develop and maintain a working relationship and foster a capacity to observe. And part of this formulation involves the therapist's current understanding about the kind of therapy his patient requires, that is, whether short-term or long-term therapy that discourages regression is most useful, or whether he has a patient who might make only minimal gains without the possibility of a regression in the psychotherapy.

For those who agree that regression in a patient in the borderline spectrum can be useful, how is the therapist to decide when a specific regression has the potential of helping—or when it can be destructive? Obviously, the distinction is very difficult to make, especially in a group of patients so expert in arousing feelings of hatred, worthlessness, helplessness, and hopelessness in the therapist. In arriving at an assessment, the therapist is always in the position of trying to observe his countertransference responses to the patient as a way of understanding the transference and to separate pathological ways that he could respond to the patient because of his countertransference. He must also evaluate the impact of the patient's regressive feelings on the latter's daily life, including frequent assessment of the patient's potential and actual self-destructiveness. Because there is probably no patient who does not spill some of the therapeutic issues into his daily life, it is hard to draw a line and say that something beyond a certain point makes the regression too self-destructive. Many therapists have had experiences with relatively healthy patients who became significantly depressed in therapy or analysis, with resultant behavior that affected their relationships and work. Yet many of these patients have ultimately benefited significantly from their treatment, leaving the therapist with the feeling that the behavioral regression was probably inevitable and necessary. At what point does the therapist say that it has gone too far? And if he chooses the "wrong" point, is he telling the patient to push away an important aspect of his life that is being analyzed and relived in the treatment?

In my experience, intense regressive feelings that appear very early in treatment have a greater potential to produce self-destructive behavioral regression. Although some workers disagree (for example, Boris 1973), a relationship with the therapist that allows the opportunity at least to define the work seems to be an important prerequisite for the emergence of therapeutically useful regressive feelings. But there are patients who bring very intense feelings immediately into the first session as their means of negotiating with the therapist. Part of the therapist's response must be based on his rapid formulation of the meaning of this patient's statements and affect, the quality of the relationship formed immediately between them, the way the patient responds to the therapist's attempts to tune in and understand, and the therapist's own comfort with the issues. Does the understanding he communicates establish a safer climate, or is the patient's life in such disorder or jeopardy that he cannot wait until the next appointment with the therapist, even if it is the next day? Implicit in this assessment is an estimate of the patient's capacity to make use of the relationship with the new therapist by means of internalization of the therapist and the therapist's relationship with the patient as a sustaining force, even though the internalization may be highly transient at first.

The therapist's assessment as to whether the regression is a defensive avoidance is another aspect related to his response to it. At times when a patient can tolerate a conflict or painful affect with support, he may nevertheless retreat into regressive behavior. The distinction is difficult but crucial; if the therapist is correct in supportively confronting his patient with the thought that the regression is an avoidance of a painful but bearable issue, his confrontation can open the way for an important piece of work. If incorrect, the confrontation tends to confirm the patient's fantasies of being misunderstood and abandoned by his therapist.

Limit setting can be used early in treatment as a way of attempting to contain a rapid regression. For example, the therapist can simply say that he is not interested in hearing about a specific area of the patient's life or feelings at present, although acknowledging its ultimate importance. Again, the correct assessment, including the therapist's comfort with certain material, often determines the success of the limit setting.

Most therapists acknowledge the importance of the therapist's personality in determining the success of the therapy. The ability of some consultants to make successful matches of patient and therapist is based on their ability to assess the personality qualities of the therapist and their "fit" with the patient's conflicts, personality, and diagnosis. Shapiro (1973) spelled out the differences between two therapists in their treatment of the same woman. The first therapist's open, warm personality, his difficulties in separating his professional from his personal life, his discomfort with his patient's anality, and his view that his patient was someone who had to be totally accepted led to a regression that appeared as a stalemate in the treatment. Her second therapist expected more of her, more clearly defined his limits, and encouraged her experimentation with her anality. His position led to significant changes in the patient's behavior coincident with his incorporation as an increasingly active person in her anal fantasies. Shapiro believes that such personality characteristics of therapists are only minimally changeable in training, and yet are a major determinant of the success of treatment with many patients.

The personality of the therapist obviously plays an important role in the nature of his countertransference fantasies, as well as in his behavioral response to them in treatment, and ultimately is related to the outcome of the regression of a specific patient. The therapist's personality is especially crucial in the treatment of the borderline group of patients, who so often establish a primitive transference involving fusion with the therapist or his idealization or devaluation. Because the core issue for many of these patients relates to the very early life-and-death, devour-or-be-devoured struggle with a maternal figure, the therapist's comfort with an intense transference of such material is crucial. It includes not only the capacity to accept the transference of the role of nurturing mother—and to give it up later—but also the ability to feel relatively secure with the ego boundary fluctuations of early periods. Projections, projective identification, and fusion phenomena of the patient can be experiences for the therapist that lead to anxiety and a tendency to withdraw, counterattack, or somatize. The therapist's capacity to accept the idealization of the patient without clarifying his human fallibility has been defined by Kohut (1968) as one of the crucial aspects in the treatment of narcissistic characters. Kohut also describes the importance of the therapist's ability to listen to a patient who is using him as a mirror for early narcissistic, grandiose fantasies without having to interpret or respond nonthera-

peutically to the boredom that he may experience in allowing such material to unfold. Kohut emphasizes that the
therapist's comfort with the primitive grandiose part of
himself makes the work with these patients possible.

One of the most difficult ingredients of a therapist's
personality to define is that of flexibility, that is, a capacity
to determine the changing needs, affects, and conflicts of
the patient and to respond to them appropriately. An
acceptance of a patient's idealization of the therapist can be
crucial early in the therapy of some of these patients. But
the persistence later in treatment of the therapist's view of
the patient as needing to idealize him may belie the therapist's wishes for precisely this type of narcissistic gratification, and retard the patient's capacity to grow. The nurturant mother transference, so important at one point, may
be something that the therapist demands later to protect
himself from the patient's fury or the patient's increasing
capacity to separate himself from the therapist. Balint
(1968) discusses the countertransference omnipotence of the
therapist as a determinant of whether regression is "be-
nign" or "malignant." This omnipotence can be manifest
when the therapist rationalizes his active giving to or
rescuing of the patient because of his own needs rather than
the patient's. The therapist's flexibility, then, has two
aspects: a basic personality attribute that he brings to his
work, coupled with a capacity to be aware of and to
tolerate his own countertransference responses before they
become actions that impede the therapeutic process. Often
it means being able to acknowledge murderous hate, envy,
or intense infantile longings in himself and to be comfortable
with this primitive material. It requires a capacity to maintain a stance that is empathic, permitting the transference to
unfold, whether murderous, idealizing, fusing, or other.

# Clinical Illustration

These issues, difficulties, and dilemmas can be illustrated by returning to the case of Ms. D., described briefly in Chapter 5. When Ms. D. underwent a profound regression in therapy, her therapist was put in the position of having to decide where he stood on regressions in general, and with this patient in particular, as well as what role his counter-transference responses played in the treatment. The patient sought help for her difficulties in forming relationships with people and completing her graduate studies. During the first few months of treatment, she was able to use her therapy as a supportive structure. She had no difficulty with the therapist's summer vacation, which occurred after a month of treatment. Over the next six months, however, she gradually began to feel desperate and empty in the treatment situation, and longed to be held constantly. What emerged was her acknowledgment that she felt furious at her therapist for not offering the amount of symbolic holding and support she believed she required. As her anger increased during a specific session, she might scream in rage and then hit her head against the wall or pound her fists against her head or thighs. Although this behavior at times terrified the therapist, he slowly became comfortable with all but the most severe outbursts. His increasing activity seemed important, especially his offers to her that she could phone him or come for extra sessions if necessary. She occasionally made use of these offers, phoning in panic but usually becoming comfortable after a five- or ten-minute conversation, with the realization that the therapist still existed and was not about to retaliate or abandon her. During one of his vacations she became seriously suicidal, requiring hospitalization until his return. All the same, most of the time she was able to continue her graduate studies with distinction.

Although outbursts of fury followed by self-punishment continued throughout the therapy, the patient gradually became able to define some of the fantasies and feelings that led to the terrifying quality of her fury. In her rage she felt that she destroyed any image of the therapist or anyone else inside of her. She also felt at those times that the therapist either hated her or ridiculed and laughed at her. No clarification of reality seemed to make any difference in the middle of these outbursts, although she could describe the details of the feelings later in the session with some realistic appreciation.

The therapist was able to relate these episodes to the repeated loss of her parents early in life, especially a long separation when she was 2 years old. He explained her feelings to her as a reexperiencing of what had been unacceptable and impossible for her to feel if she was to survive within her family. At first she thought the therapist was imposing an explanation on her that did not relieve her immediate panic, but gradually she could make use of it as something of her own.

Several areas of change became apparent over the four years of therapy. Within the sessions the patient gradually came to feel more comfortable with her anger at the therapist and could even leave the hour feeling angry at him without losing the sense that he existed. She could occasionally have angry fantasies about him when not in his office, which previously would have been intolerable and would have led to panic. There was also an increasing ability to relate to the therapist with warmth and a sense of being more of a whole person. In her daily life, relationships with men became more satisfying. Instead of reliving the drama with them that was played out in her sessions, she gradually learned to contain her intense feelings and bring them into therapy. To her surprise, she found it gratifying to behave in a more mature way and learned that her infantile needs were not so intense as to require constant gratification. She also experienced periods in which she felt that she had a "self" and did not have to be held all the time.

The treatment of such a patient can be a frightening experience to a patient and therapist, with many risks, including the possibility of suicide. As described earlier, a constant danger in the outpatient therapy with such patients is the possibility that regression during the therapy hour will spill over into the patient's life. The therapist's understanding, personality, and technical skill can help keep the regression confined largely to the therapy sessions with most of these patients, and can serve to structure it in such a way as to allow the patient to experience therapy with a greater sense of safety.

Suggestion, for example, is often a helpful technique in confining regression to the therapy hour, as illustrated by the case of Ms. D. When the patient was able to contain her feelings in her relationships with men, she was often liable to intense outbursts of affect in therapy. The therapist would then remind her, in part as a way of reminding himself, that she had done as agreed in not disrupting outside relationships between appointments. This also helped the therapist tolerate Ms. D.'s fury by allowing him to see it in terms of a theoretical model that limited acting out and brought the conflicts and feelings into therapy.

Extremely important in limiting a patient's regression is the therapist's basic position about his own omnipotence: his need to rescue his patients and receive adulation and narcissistic gratification from them. I have already discussed some of the relevant countertransference and personality factors involved. The therapist's acceptance of his human limitations without shame or guilt can help him find appropriate ways to clarify the extent of his capacity to be available to his patient. In an example from Ms. D.'s treatment, she became frightened that she might call her therapist on the phone more and more in her insatiable hunger and greed until he finally became angry at her and ultimately rejected her. Although the therapist was aware of a part of himself that had a similar concern, he replied that up to that time she had not called so often as to infringe upon his personal life. If she did he would let her know and would view it as a signal from her that she needed more structure. He would then consider hospitalization. He reminded her that he had hospitalized her in the past and had continued to see her while she was there. If she required hospitalization, he would certainly be available for appointments and would work with her as an inpatient until she was sufficiently comfortable with her relationship with him and her capacity to control her feelings as an outpatient. She found these remarks reassuring; her fury and fear of abandonment and rejection temporarily became less intense following them.

These vignettes also illustrate the use of limit setting in psychotherapy. If a therapist accepts his human limitations, he also defines the limits he feels are tolerable and appropriate in the therapeutic situation. In the light of his personality and his theoretical model of what is useful in psychotherapy, he constantly assesses these limits. When the therapist feels he has to take a firmer position, he must always consider the role his countertransference rage and wishes to retaliate may play, since the need for limit setting often occurs at a time when the patient is being provocatively furious. Sometimes his limits are based on countertransference difficulties that may be rationalized as theoretical issues. The therapist in the case of Ms. D., for example, was tempted to state that his patient's outbursts were so disruptive and disorganizing for her that she would have to control them more within the sessions. In looking at the matter further, however, he concluded that it was his own anxiety during the outbursts that was the major factor in his wish that she limit them. Nor does limit setting always have to be a firm statement to the patient to stop some behavior; it can also be couched as an expression of the therapist's concern. For many patients this concern is evidence that the therapist cares, and stands in sharp contrast to earlier experiences of significant neglect.

Even though patients in the borderline spectrum have serious difficulties in establishing an observing ego and maintaining even a tenuous working relationship, an approach that emphasizes the therapist's attention to these defects can help contain a regression. Clearly the therapist has to believe that it is possible to help the patient develop these capacities. On some level the patient must maintain an awareness of the therapist's constant attempts to share with him the assessment of the current situation and to help him observe the meaning of certain feelings and behavior. It took many months for Ms. D. to be able to look at the meaning of her regressive behavior, but relatively rapidly she could share with her therapist an assessment of her suicidal potential between sessions in a way that emphasized the collaborative aspects of her treatment.

The clarification of reality is also crucial during regressive episodes. The therapist may need to state that he is angry with his patient if he senses that his anger is perceived by the patient and is interfering with the treatment. In addition to this clarification, the therapist can ultimately help the patient explore what there was about his behavior that could have provoked the therapist to anger. Reality clarification also includes helping the patient be aware of the distortions and projections in the transference and in relationships with others.

Finally, many of these patients require help in learning to relate to people that can best be categorized as education. This type of education can sometimes short circuit the disruptive aspects of an infantile regressive transference. With Ms. D. the therapist spent many hours discussing her graduate studies, her ways of relating to classmates and the students she taught, in an approach that focused on how people spoke to one another, felt about one another, and related to one another. The danger exists, of course, that the therapist can assume an authoritarian role in such discussions that may support a regressive transference rather than limit it. In addition, he can continue such work as an avoidance of anxiety-laden issues that both he and the patient are reluctant to face.

It is easier to talk about models of treatment that define ideal therapists than to face realistically that such therapists exist only in the fantasies of patients and their therapists. Since there are obviously many therapists who work effectively with patients, we have to define the balance of qualities necessary to make good therapy possible. The "good-enough" therapist does make mistakes. But his errors are rarely the serious acting out of destructive counter-transference fantasies. On balance, his caring, concern, devotion, and understanding outweigh his errors. Just as the child senses the basic caring and respect of the good-enough mother even when she fails, so does the patient accept and forgive honest mistakes and lapses when the balance resides on the side of an effort to understand and work with him effectively.

# Ten

# Devaluation and Countertransference

In this chapter I shall discuss the countertransference responses of the therapist to the devaluing borderline patient. To the extent that devaluation contributes, from the patient's side, to the characteristic feelings of helplessness and hopelessness of the therapist in borderline psychotherapy, it represents, in microcosm, the constellation of issues that therapists must confront in their work with such patients.

## Devaluation

Devaluation of the therapist is a frequent manifestation of many of the pathological defenses and character styles of borderline patients. It can take the form of belittling the therapist verbally about his manner, appearance, understanding, skill, or intelligence. He can be contrasted negatively with previous therapists or consultants. Nonverbally, devaluation may be manifested in treating the therapist as inanimate or not present in the room (Searles 1963). Such patients may never greet the therapist or allow any conversation that acknowledges him as a human being. They may respond to the therapist's clarifications and interpretations as if they were never spoken, continuing with what they were saying before they were interrupted. Some patients use action to demonstrate their devaluation. They may miss appointments, come late, leave treatment, or commit some antisocial act that takes them away from the therapist. The verbal and nonverbal behavior by the patient communicates many things; among them is the message "You are worth nothing to me and have nothing to offer me. You may think that you have some way to help me, but I am showing that you are valueless and do not."

There are many motivations that lead to this devaluation of the therapist as an end result. I shall enumerate some, with the understanding that I am separating processes that intertwine and overlap.

AN EXPRESSION OF RAGE

We have already seen that the borderline patient anticipates rejection and tends to interpret anything except unconditional giving as an abandonment. The expression of rage, therefore, appears in therapy after experiences of fantasied rejection, or after the therapist is unable to gratify the patient's unrealistic expectations. The patient often uses devaluation to express his rage that the therapist is not the warm source of nurturance he had wished for.

A 30-year-old accountant came into treatment because of his loneliness and inability to have satisfactory prolonged relationships. He quickly revealed his difficulties in therapy by maintaining an aloof, supercilious air, rarely looking at the therapist and belittling any clarifications. The therapist began to focus on this patient's aloofness as a protection against underlying anger when he did not get the comforting he wanted from the therapist. Gradually the patient became increasingly angry, verbally attacking the therapist for his incompetence and weakness, and then had the frightening experience of feeling himself and the therapist turning into apes who would destroy each other.

PROTECTION AGAINST WISHES FOR NURTURANCE

The longings and wishes for closeness, love, and nurturance that these patients experience are terrifying to them. Such feelings bring up concerns about being disappointed, helpless, and abandoned. In some patients these wishes may threaten regression, with the felt threat of annihilation. If the therapist has little worth to the patient and the therapeutic situation little to offer him, the patient can deny his intense longings. As the patient in this situation begins to be aware of his increasing involvement, devaluation of the therapist protects him against the feared disappointment or regression. At the same time, devaluation symbolically represents a defensive refusal to take in what is so intensely longed for.

The patient just described gradually became aware, mainly through dreams, of his wishes to be held and nursed by the therapist. After a period of increasing attacks, consisting of complaints that the therapist was weak, feminine, and stupid and lacked an understanding of the problems involved, the patient had a fantasy that he was like a sea lamprey, wanting to hang onto the therapist, never let go, and suck forever. From that moment he could see spontaneously that he would have to attack and belittle the therapist to keep such fantasies from consciousness.

PROTECTION AGAINST ENVY

Akin to affectionate longings for the therapist is an intense envy of him and a wish to swallow him whole and be like him. Such envy may arouse so much discomfort in the patient that devaluing the therapist feels like his only means of protection; there is nothing to envy and engulf if the therapist is valueless.

A 31-year-old engineer, early in analysis, saw the analyst as a helpful person but had intermittent paranoid fears that the analyst would exploit him, take his money, and change him. After one year of treatment the patient reported a series of dreams: The first was about a group of nurses having a lunch of round doughy things topped with whipped cream and a red cherry. The succeeding dreams became explicit seductions of compliant women in which the patient would fondle or suck their breasts. Concomitant with these dreams, whose oral transference implications were spelled out to the patient, were days of increasing attacks on the analyst for not understanding him and having nothing good to offer, as well as feelings that analysis was useless and not the solution to his problems. After several sessions of analyzing this material, the patient discussed the devaluation as a protection against his wishes to suck. In addition, he then spoke of his envy of how much the analyst had and could give to him and other patients.

PROTECTION AGAINST PROJECTED ANGER

A therapist who is valued is often felt by borderline patients to be dangerous and retaliatory, because their anger may be projected onto him. The therapist seen as weak, helpless, and worthless cannot destroy the patient.

A 21-year-old waitress, described by a colleague as "The Black Death" to capture the feeling of her intense, chronic rage and depression, repeatedly minimized the importance of the therapist, the value of his comments, and his ability to care about and help her. Early in therapy there occurred several episodes of increasing anger, immediately followed by intensely fearful outbursts that the therapist hated her and would throw her out or physically injure her. She then returned to belittling the therapist and the therapeutic relationship to protect herself against her fury and her need to project it onto the therapist.

## PROJECTION OF LOW SELF-ESTEEM

Borderline patients invariably have extremely low self-esteem. Its components often are related to the patients' feelings about their inability to control their fury or the unacceptability of their infantile longings. They may attempt to rid themselves of such feelings by placing them in the therapist. This displacement can be expressed in the devaluation of the therapist, sometimes resulting in the patient's feeling more worthwhile.

A 45-year-old single bookkeeper suffered from years of chronic depression and isolation; she began working again in order to pay for her therapy after several years of serious withdrawal. In therapy, after weeks of crying and virtual silence, she spoke of her worthlessness, emptiness, inability to give anything to anyone, and hopelessness. Her discussion of these feelings was characterized by little affect except for that associated with her repeated attacks on the therapist. He was described as a worthless, useless person who could not give her anything, not even pills. At times she would storm out of the office angrily, but on other occasions she appeared more relaxed and friendly after these repetitive barrages.

## A TRANSFERENCE MANIFESTATION

Borderline patients may be reliving real or fantasied devaluation by a parent in the transference. By identification with the devaluing parent, they become that parent and treat the therapist as they themselves felt treated in childhood.

The 21-year-old waitress described earlier had seriously disturbed parents who reacted to her as an inferior version of a brother who died shortly after she was born. In the analysis of the transference, it became clear that she expected her therapist to see her as his most inferior patient. She also recognized that she belittled the therapist in the way her parents belittled her.

The personality and skills of the therapist are particularly crucial in working with this group of patients. The capacity to develop trusting and loving relationships with people, so lacking initially in these patients, is related to the process of internalization of the good therapist who himself demonstrates these capacities in his work with the patient. As already suggested, the chief experiences that permit this process to occur are repeated encounters with the patient's anger in therapy. The therapist's consistent, tactful, non-retaliatory handling of the patient's rage allows pathological defenses to be given up slowly and permits the patient to experience the therapist as the truly good object who can safely be introjected. The therapist's appropriate response to the patient's anger gradually provides the patient with the knowledge that he can feel intimate and helpless with the therapist without being swallowed, even though he and even the therapist may wish for it.

The verbal expression of anger in psychotherapy provides the patient with the possibility of a new kind of experience. He can experience and ultimately learn that he can verbalize anger, not act on it, not destroy the therapist, not have the therapist retaliate, and not be rejected or abandoned by the therapist. This repeated encounter thus provides a model for identification that helps the patient develop new ego capacities. Once it is safe to verbalize anger, the patient and therapist can investigate more readily the meaning of its presence at a particular moment and its origins, all of which are important in the resolution of the patient's rage.

## Countertransference and Self-Psychology

Among the many contributions of self-psychology is its recognition that selfobject needs exist in all people to varying degrees throughout their lives. Relatively mature therapists and analysts require some validation from their patients that they are competent, effective clinicians. They receive this validation from experiences of understanding their patients and being useful to them, from the realization that the functions they perform for their patients ultimately lead to their patients' growth. As long as the patient uses his therapist and responds to him sufficiently to confirm his competence, the therapist will maintain a solid, comfortable feeling about himself as someone of worth and value. But when the therapist has one or more borderline patients who devalue, reject, or deny his attempts to help, consistent with the nature of their emerging transference, the therapist may then find himself feeling very much as the patient does.

The therapist's despair and anger can be viewed as a response to his own experience of feeling that he has failed as a selfobject; that is, he does not appear to be performing the selfobject functions that the patient says he wants from him. Usually unrecognized by both patient and therapist are the silent (and therefore often preconscious or unconscious) holding selfobject transferences that provide the stability necessary to permit unresolved issues of the past to emerge. Disappointment, despair, and anger from the past are thus reactivated and relived in the transference. They elicit countertransference responses in the therapist to the extent that they involve him as the failing selfobject recreated from the patient's past failing selfobjects. Because neither the patient nor therapist is in touch with the positive self-object bond that allows these feelings to emerge, both experience pain in the transference-countertransference. The patient feels helpless and hopeless in the transference; the therapist, because he cannot soothe, satisfy, adequately understand, or help the patient (from both his and the patient's perspective), experiences the situation as his own failure. When chronically repeated, this experience ultimately relates to the therapist's failure to receive the valida-tion of his professional competence that he requires. A paradox of this transference-countertransference situation is that, in the *successful* transference reliving, the therapist experiences his failure as a selfobject only after he has first succeeded as a holding selfobject; the patient in turn, in experiencing the therapist as the failing selfobject, fails the therapist by not performing the selfobject validating func-tion that the therapist intermittently needs. (This should not be taken to mean that it is the patient's *task* to perform this validating function, only that when at such times the patient does not validate the therapist's sense of competence suffi-ciently, the described countertransference experiences are usually inevitable.)

When the therapist can view his countertransference experience as his empathic response to the feelings of his patient, he has a clue to the nature of the patient's current and past experiences. But it is not easy to maintain a balance between immersion in the patient's feelings and the requisite distance from them necessary to function most effectively as therapist and selfobject. The task is particu-larly difficult to the extent that the therapist's intense countertransference experiences include a transient or more prolonged conviction that he indeed does not understand, or that he lacks an adequate empathic capacity with, this specific patient. He may, as described, question what he previously felt were solidly established aspects of his own self and his therapeutic skills. Are the patient's feelings of hopelessness, rage, and rejection of the therapist the reliving in the transference of early selfobject failures? Are they being experienced in response to the expectable failures of a good to excellent selfobject therapist? Or has the therapist indeed failed the patient because of his significant empathic limitations or countertransference difficulties with the specific patient? The therapist's ability to raise these questions puts him in a good position to examine the various possibilities as he continues his work with the patient. Sometimes consultations with a trusted and respected colleague are necessary to sort out these complex issues and gain some perspective.

## Countertransference Responses to Devaluing Patients

What does it feel like to sit with the patient who repeatedly devalues us? The experience can be devastating, especially for the young therapist. It may arouse feelings of intense worthlessness and depression, fear, rage, guilt, shame, and envy. The therapist may turn his rage against himself if he feels guilty about it, intensifying his depression. He may feel guilt and shame that he cannot rescue the patient and live up to the patient's expectations that he be the omnipotent parent. He is particularly vulnerable to feeling shame when he is confronted with his all-too-human response of envy to the patient's demands for unconditional care and nurturance.

The young therapist especially may respond to persistent devaluation by these patients with a temporary, sometimes prolonged regression that exposes his doubts, not only about his abilities, but as to whether working with a patient in a theoretical model that values verbal interchange is at all helpful. He is particularly vulnerable to the patient who tells him that his professional and personal doubts are correct. These patients are expert in perceiving aspects of the therapist's personality that are problem areas for the therapist. Primitive patients probably develop this skill from their style of existence, in which every encounter with any person is so threatening that they must perceive his weaknesses in order to be prepared for the final battle for survival.

I shall now discuss the various ways that the therapist may respond to these devaluing, angry attacks.

WITHDRAWAL

I have already outlined how these verbal attacks may leave the therapist feeling personally hurt, angry, or hopeless. His behavioral response to these feelings may be withdrawal. He may stop listening to the patient, daydream about something else, or feel bored or angry. He may have conscious wishes that the patient leave treatment. This withdrawal may be manifested in his nonintervention when a clarification or interpretation would be useful. These sensitive patients will intuitively feel the therapist's withdrawal and often respond with increasing concerns about rejection and abandonment. They may either become angrier or passively compliant in order not to lose their therapist completely.

When the patient complains that his therapist is less available as a caring, interested person, the therapist may have a ready explanation to support his withdrawal. Especially manifest in the beginning therapist is his use of the defense that he is being a good, nondirective psychotherapist. Therapists often start their training attempting to fulfill a fantasy of what the psychoanalytic model of treatment is, including the fantasy of the mirrorlike image of the analyst. The therapist's retreat into this fantasied identification often masks his fear, anger, depression, or hopelessness when confronted with a difficult and threatening patient. An example of such behavior was a therapist working in a prison with an angry, devaluing, frightening inmate. This patient wanted to shake hands with him at the end of the meetings. The therapist refused, feeling that he was gratifying the patient too much rather than analyzing what the patient's wish meant.

The therapist's withdrawal may be manifested in the ways he allows the patient to devalue their work within the therapeutic sessions by not pursuing actively the meaning of lateness, missed appointments, or nonpayment of bills.

Withdrawal can lead to very serious consequences when it involves the therapist's reluctance to intervene in destructive or self-destructive activities of the patient outside the therapeutic setting. The patient may be communicating that he is out of control, or may be testing to see whether the therapist cares enough for him to prevent him from doing anything destructive to himself or the important people in his life. The nonintervention by the therapist at this point is often felt by the patient as confirmation of his fears that the therapist does not care about him.

DEFENDING HIMSELF

The therapist may respond to repeated attacks by defending himself, telling the patient that he knows what he is doing and has worth and something to offer. As part of this response he may point out to the patient the progress they have made and how much better the patient is in certain ways. The defensive nature of this position is evident to the patient, who may respond with increasing anger and anxiety, or with compliance and suppression of anger.

## PROVING HIS OMNIPOTENCE AND LOVE

The therapist can respond to the patient's provocations by active demonstrations that he loves the patient, has the magical supplies the patient demands, and is the omnipotent, giving, rescuing parent. He may tell the patient he cares about him, terrifying him by the threat this presents to his tenuous autonomy. He may give and smother symbolically or actually, sometimes making the patient feel content momentarily but often frightening the patient, who has a part of him that knows that such gratification of his primitive demands is no solution and will only make him feel more helpless and worthless.

## RETALIATING

A common outcome of attacks by these patients is retaliation by the therapist. Its manifestations may be mild, as in teasing or subtle criticism, or overtly angry and rejecting. It may take the form of interpreting the patient's feelings of entitlement, not as part of the therapist's commitment to the selfobject transference, but as an angry counterattack involving envy of the patient's feelings. This is not to say that the anger of the therapist is not a useful tool, but when it is used to reject the patient, it is extremely destructive. It intensifies the distrust already present and ruptures the tenuous working relationship.

## INTERPRETING THE ANGER AS MASKING LOVE

The therapist may be so uncomfortable with the repeated angry attacks that he unconsciously defends himself by deciding that they are masking feelings of love and closeness that the patient cannot accept. Sometimes, of course, this is true. But if the issue for the patient is really his murderous rage, the therapist's incorrect interpretation will tell him that the therapist cannot tolerate it.

## Clinical Illustration

Some of these points can be illustrated with reference to the 30-year-old accountant described briefly at the beginning of this chapter. Because I am concerned here so largely with countertransference issues, and wish to emphasize the personal quality of the therapist's responses, I shall use the first-person throughout this account.

Mr. F. was of average height, thin, awkward, and adolescent in his gestures and voice. His sitting position from the start was characteristic of the way in which he related to me for years: He would slouch and practically lie on the chair, talking to the overhead lighting fixture, the picture to the left of my head, or the window to the right. He spoke with a soft southern drawl in an aloof way, yet at the same time he could summon up articulate and bitingly humorous descriptions of his work, his past, and the few people in his current world. He could readily define the major disappointments in his life that had determined his responses to people ever since: His mother, who had held, hugged, and hovered over him for the first five years of his life, had abandoned him for his newborn sister. To him it had felt like being an infant suddenly thrown off his mother's lap. He had tried to woo her back by adopting her loving, smiling fundamentalist religious position, which included a denial of jealousy or anger. He had also tried turning to his brusque, busy father, who scorned him for his awkwardness and weakness. He struggled to love but at the same time found himself vomiting up the lunches his mother had packed for him to eat in school. Gradually he began to vomit the food he ate at home. His friendships at school were jeopardized by his need to report to his mother the nasty things the other children said and did; he agreed with her that he would never think such naughty thoughts himself. During his adolescence he became increasingly preoccupied with thoughts of inadvertently hurting people, which culminated in marked anxiety in his early twenties when he became afraid that he would stab pregnant women in the abdomen. This anxiety led him to his college health service and his first experience with psychotherapy.

In spite of these difficulties, he did well academically in high school, spent two years in the navy, where he felt liberated, and was able to complete college successfully. His relationships with women consisted of looking at them from afar, actively fantasying closeness and hugging; actual contacts were awkward and brief. He could form more sustained but still distant relationships with men. He was transiently concerned that he might be a homosexual at the time he was discharged from the navy.

His first psychotherapy occurred during his last year at college. He had felt frightened and desperate and had quickly come to see his therapist as the man who had rescued him. His therapist was a psychiatric resident whom the patient described as large, athletic "like a football player," a smoker of big cigars who actively gave advice and was very real and direct with him. In looking back at this therapy, my patient felt that it had helped to diminish his preoccupations and anxieties but had left him still unable to form lasting, satisfying relationships with people. It had ended before he felt ready, because his therapist, after one year of work with the patient, had finished his training and left the area. When I first saw the patient six years later, he defined his problem as a chronic one that he felt he could not solve alone. Yet he felt pessimistic that anything could be done to change things.

This patient was one of my first private patients and really puzzled me. I was impressed by his wish to work, on the one hand, and by his loneliness and isolation, and the frightening quality of his anger, on the other. I was concerned about his aloofness and distance from me; I did not feel that he and I were making contact with each other, but I did not know what to do about it either. At that point in my experience, I could not even formulate the question of how much I liked him and whether that was important. I did recognize that he had a choice of whether he wished to see me regularly, and I offered him that opportunity at the end of our first meeting. He replied that he was willing to see me and felt that one hour a week was what he had in mind.

From my perception of the first few months of our meetings, nothing much happened. He gave me more history to fill out the outline of his life and told me more about the emptiness of his current existence, but all in a manner that shut me out and maintained an amused distance. He became a patient about whom I would sigh wearily before inviting him in. Because of my distress and increasing boredom, I began to point out as tactfully as I could the way he was avoiding contact with me and keeping me out of his world. His response over a number of months, with an insistent sameness, was a quick glance followed by the sad admission that he had made a mistake. He did not know how to tell me, but I was not the right therapist for him. In addition to my soft voice and mild manner, I probably had never been in a bar in my life, had never been in a fist fight, and did not smoke cigars. He would then speak with affection about his previous therapist and again spell out the vast differences between us.

When I could recover from what occasionally felt like a devastating personal attack, I would try to help him look at the meaning of what he was saying. I would relate it to his relationship with his mother, his fury at her abandoning him and his wish to turn to the other parent, who also let him down; often I could point to specific parallels. Usually he rejected these interpretations as incorrect, irrelevant, and worthless. He would also deny that he felt any anger at me when I would point out the obvious attacking quality of many of his statements. How could he be angry when he wasn't even involved and didn't care, he would reply.

Over a nine-month period I went through stages of boredom, withdrawal, fury, depression, and helplessness. I gradually began to feel like a broken record. I had run out of new ideas, and I found myself increasingly willing to acknowledge that maybe he was right: I probably was not the therapist for him. With relief I suggested that he see a consultant, who would help us make that determination. I also had to acknowledge to myself that my narcissism was on the line. To fail with one of my first private patients, and because of so many alleged personal inadequacies, was more than I wished to face at that time. Also, I had chosen a consultant I greatly respected, adding to my concerns about revealing my inadequacies as a therapist.

The consultant felt that therapy had certainly been stalemated, but largely because of the infrequency of the visits and the lack of confidence I had in the worth of my work with the patient. He minimized my insistence that the patient did not feel I was the right therapist. He stated that in his interview with the patient, the patient had talked about what he did not like but also conveyed a respect for our work and some willingness to continue with me. After the consultation I ambivalently negotiated with this patient for psychoanalytic treatment involving the use of the couch and five meetings a week. With the reassurance that at least my consultant loved me, I arranged to have the consultant continue as my supervisor.

Psychoanalysis with this patient lasted four years. The position he took in our earlier therapy was maintained but this time amplified and understood by means of dreams and memories that verified previous hypotheses. Clarifications about his murderous rage that appeared in dreams made it somewhat safer to talk about his fury with me. Gradually he could speak intellectually about the possibility of an involvement with me, but it was something he never really felt. Only on two occasions did he actually express anger toward me, both leading to near disruption of the analysis. One followed my inflexibility when he wanted to change an appointment, and led to his calling the consultant in order to request a change of analysts. The other occurred toward the end of analysis, when I pointed out his need to maintain a paranoid position in relation to people. It resulted in his storming out of the hour and phoning that he was never returning. He came back after one missed session. Gradually, I became personally more comfortable with this patient, although seeing him was always hard work. I felt much less helpless and hopeless as I came to see his attacks, isolation, and distance in the context of a theoretical framework and as part of the transference and defense against it. My supervisor's support and clarifications helped me to maintain this distance. But my helplessness was still present when my interpretations were rejected for long periods of time and I was treated as some nonhuman appendage to my chair. I often felt hopeless that we would ever achieve the goals we had set. I say "we," but usually it felt like "I" and "him," with little sense of our working together. I frequently had to ask myself whether I liked him enough to suffer with him all those years, but I had to acknowledge grudgingly that in spite of everything, I did. Somehow the process of long-term work with him had made me feel like a parent with a difficult child, a parent who could finally come to accept any change at all in that child with happiness. The changes that occurred were presented to me casually. They consisted of passing comments about his increasing ability to date women, and led ultimately to his marrying a woman with whom he could share mutual tenderness.

I believe that certain aspects of this patient's defensive structure and the transference that emerged in analysis made working with him particularly difficult for me. He was reliving a relationship of helplessness and hopelessness with his mother. Not only did he feel abandoned by her when his sister was born, but he was allowed no direct way to express the anger and jealousy he experienced. He chose to comply on the surface but maintained an aloof, disparaging distance from her that protected him against his fury, helplessness, and despair. Because he did this with his mother to stay alive, he understandably repeated the same pattern with me, complying on the surface but vomiting up and rejecting what I attempted to give. In a sense he never left that position with me; he was able to change the quality of relationships outside of analysis but maintained his aloofness with me to the end. He would say that to show real change with me was to acknowledge that he had taken something from me and kept it as part of himself; he just did not want to do that openly, for he would have to admit the importance of our relationship and how grateful he was. His compromise was to remain very much the same with me, to change significantly outside, and then to ascribe the changes to things he could take from the new important people in his life.

# PART THREE
# Other Treatment Issues

--------------------Eleven--------------------

# Hospital Management

Hospital treatment of borderline patients may be indicated during regressions marked by increasingly destructive or self-destructive behavior. In this chapter I shall deal with aspects of the hospital treatment of all borderline patients but shall emphasize those patients already in therapy who require hospitalization during ongoing treatment. I shall stress (1) unresolved developmental issues that emerge in therapy and that require more support than that available to the patient outside the hospital; (2) useful functions hospitalization can perform for both patient and therapist; (3) the therapist's countertransference difficulties and vulnerabilities, which may become more manifest when the patient is hospitalized; (4) hospital staff countertransference difficulties that promote destructive, regressive patient behavior and that may often impede the therapist's work with the patient; and (5) administrative and staff problems within the hospital setting that can facilitate or impede the resolution of issues that led to hospitalization.

# Indications for Hospitalization

Hospitalization has to be considered for borderline patients who are experiencing intense panic and emptiness, either because of the emergence of destructive fury in the transference or because of a desperate reaction to relative or total loss of important people or other disappointments in their current lives. Implicit in this desperation is an inability to experience the therapist as someone who constantly exists, who is available and supportive. The fragile, unstable working relationship characteristic of borderline patients readily breaks down under stress. The patient's desperation may include destructive and self-destructive preoccupations and present a serious danger of suicide and other destructive or self-destructive behavior.

Treatment of borderline patients within a hospital setting provides the patient and treatment team, including the patient's therapist, with a series of opportunities to formulate and implement a treatment plan leading to a productive use of hospitalization, rather than one that supports and continues the regressive behavior, with its real dangers. Whether the borderline patient requires and can benefit from hospitalization depends upon an evaluation of several factors: the patient's basic ego strengths and ego weaknesses, the type or types of precipitating stress, the support systems available to the patient outside the hospital, the patient's relation to his therapist, the intensity of the transference feelings, and the therapist's awareness of his countertransference feelings and responses. Also important are the quality and availability of an appropriate hospital, the patient's and family's willingness to participate in the hospitalization, and the financial resources of the patient and family, including the adequacy of hospitalization insurance.

Because hospitalization may be the first stable situation in a long time for a desperate, disorganized borderline patient, it may also provide the first opportunity for the patient to collaborate in a thorough evaluation. This evaluation should include participation of the family and a careful look at the patient's work with his therapist. Even though the therapist who hospitalizes the patient has attempted to evaluate the needs and usefulness of hospitalization, this outpatient evaluation may of necessity be brief and sketchy because of the chaos of the patient's life and the dangers the patient is facing. On the other hand, patients who decompensate during long-term therapy may have been thoroughly evaluated by their therapist. Hospitalization for this group offers a chance for the therapist to obtain an impartial evaluation of his work with the patient, assistance with the family if indicated, and a safe setting to begin the resolution of transference issues that overwhelm the patient.

Once the decision to hospitalize the patient is made, the choice of hospital is important. When there are several suitable hospitals in which the staff has a dynamic understanding of programs for the borderline patient, considerations include the need for short- or long-term hospitalization, whether the therapist can continue with the patient while the patient is in the hospital, whether the hospital's policy supports this continued psychotherapeutic work, and whether, in cases in which it is indicated, the hospital emphasizes family involvement.

## The Hospital Setting: A Good-Enough Mothering and Holding Environment

The borderline patient's developmental vulnerabilities must be addressed in the hospital setting. The regressed suicidal or destructive patient requires a protective environment that fulfills many aspects of Winnicott's (1965) "holding environment" and has a staff with the characteristics of his "good-enough mothering" concept. The abandoned-child feelings of the enraged, regressed borderline patient are accompanied by distrust, panic, and a feeling of nonsupport and desperation. The transient loss of an evocative memory capacity for important sustaining people contributes significantly to feelings of being "dropped," alone, abandoned, and isolated, and the panic these feelings induce.

When borderline patients require hospitalization, the ward structure must provide holding qualities that offer the needed soothing and security. A sufficient empathic staff response to the patient's rage, despair, and aloneness provides the potential for relationships with new people who can communicate their grasp of the patient's experience with them and be physically present and empathically available often enough. Holding and good-enough mothering imply a genuine flexibility; the child at different ages and with different experiences and stresses needs a varying response from caring parental figures. The highest level of expression of these functions by a hospital staff includes the understanding that the borderline patient is an adult who may be transiently overwhelmed; the adult aspects require nurturance, support, and respect at the same time that the childhood vulnerabilities that have unfolded need an empathic response, which includes, when necessary, a protective response.

The "good-enough mothering" and "holding environment" concepts are often misinterpreted by the staff to mean a position that offers only a constant warm, nurturing response to all patients all the time. Such a staff response may increase the patient's regressive feelings and behavior. This misunderstanding highlights problems of utilizing early child development concepts for adult patients with difficulties that include regressions or fixations to issues related to these early years. Winnicott's concepts, when applied to hospitalized adult borderline patients, must specifically include an empathic awareness and response to adult strengths and self-esteem issues. A misunderstanding of these concepts may be part of a countertransference response that includes an omnipotent wish to rescue the patient. The correct utilization of these concepts helps support the formation of alliances and an observing ego through staff attempts to clarify and share with the patient their assessment of his complex feelings, the fluctuations of these feelings, and the patient's varying capacity to collaborate with the staff to control them over time.

The newly hospitalized borderline patient requires a rapid evaluation on admission that assesses his needs for protection. This initial evaluation investigates the suicidal and destructive dangers, and reviews the patient's history of dangerous actions in the recent and more distant past. It also includes a beginning understanding of the precipitants that led to hospitalization, as well as an evaluation of the patient's work with his therapist, if he is in therapy. A history of recent losses, whether fantasied or real, including the transient or permanent loss of a therapist, is particularly important, even though some losses may ultimately be understood as fantasied distortions or aspects of projective identification. The staff evaluation makes use of the patient's capacity to give a history, his ability to share fears and fantasies, and the degree to which he can collaborate with the staff to determine a useful hospital treatment plan. Obviously, the early assessment is very tentative, since some borderline patients have a capacity, even when regressed, to present a "false self" picture that minimizes current desperation and dangers. A staff experienced in handling borderline patients will use its empathically based countertransference fantasies and feelings as part of the assessment.

The protective and supportive measures a hospital and its staff formulate and implement, when the patient's needs are assessed correctly, can provide the most supportive holding response to an overwhelmed, regressed borderline patient. A patient may respond with a dramatic decrease in panic when his frightening suicidal feelings are evaluated to be nearly out of control and appropriate measures are instituted. These may range from assignment to a locked ward, frequent staff checks, or the assignment of a special nurse, to the use of antipsychotic medication when there is evidence of disorganization or fragmentation as a manifestation of the patient's anxiety. Again, the frequent collaborative attempts with the patient to reassess his status support the patient as someone who has strengths and the capacity to form working relationships, even though these may be transiently lost.

Once the basic protective needs of the patient are met, a more intensive, thorough evaluation of the patient and family can occur, and a treatment plan developed that includes milieu, family, and individual treatment decisions. This assessment leads to a more definitive treatment plan and helps determine whether short- or long-term hospitalization is indicated.

In the past decade many general hospitals have opened short-term intensive treatment units capable of providing excellent brief therapeutic intervention with borderline patients and their families. Such units sometimes believe they have failed when they cannot discharge a borderline patient as "improved" within weeks. They do not recognize that some borderline patients require long-term hospitalization because of long-standing ego weaknesses, overwhelming recent loss, or a family situation that has become increasingly chaotic. Kernberg (1973b) has defined characteristics of patients who require long-term hospitalization; these include low motivation for treatment, severe ego weakness as manifested by lack of anxiety tolerance and impulse control, and poor object relations. In addition, long-term inpatient hospitalization sometimes becomes a necessity because of the lack of alternatives to such hospitalization, such as day or night hospitals or halfway houses.

There are advantages and disadvantages to both short- and long-term units. A short-term hospital presents the expectation to the patient that he can resolve his regressive behavior rapidly. It also discourages new regressive behavior as an attempt to relieve distress, because the patient knows he cannot expect a long stay. Often short-term units discharge or threaten to discharge or transfer to long-term facilities those patients who regress after brief hospitalization. The knowledge of this discharge or transfer policy tends to discourage regressions; the patient may, however, utilize it for a sadomasochistic struggle with the staff or as a way of confirming projections of rage, which are then experienced as angry rejections by the staff. In addition, the patient described by Kernberg as needing long-term hospitalization may feel more misunderstood and abandoned in a setting that expects him to accomplish something beyond his capacity. The policy of discharging patients who regress is especially potentially destructive if it is part of a staff's countertransference, angry, rejecting response to the projective identifications used by the enraged, regressed borderline patient (Hartocollis 1969). When such a policy is an aspect of supportive limit setting that acknowledges realistic expectations and limits, it can be useful for those patients who can benefit from brief hospitalization. These patients may make good use of a short-term unit after discharge through a later readmission that carefully defines workable guidelines, including limits, and patient and staff expectations.

Although a long-term hospital may tend to prolong hospitalization unnecessarily for some patients, it can present a safe, supportive structure for the appropriate patient to do important work on issues of vulnerability or the precipitating stresses that led to hospitalization. For some patients it provides the required safety for the beginning resolution of the life-and-death issues that have emerged in the transference in psychotherapy. Long-term hospitalization also allows milieu aspects to be utilized more creatively than is possible in short-term settings. For example, a variety of therapy groups can flourish when the patient population is relatively stable, in contrast to the disorganizing effect of rapid group member turnover in brief hospitalization.

As Bion (1961) and Kernberg (1973a) have indicated, open-ended groups that offer little task structure tend to be regressive experiences for the participants. These regressive phenomena occur in both hospitalized borderline patients and normal populations in situations in which group tasks are left vague or undefined. This knowledge can be used in planning group experiences for a hospitalized borderline patient. A program of specific task groups, as in community and ward meetings and occupational therapy, and less structured experiences, such as those of psychotherapy groups, can be defined to fulfill the needs of each patient. It may be that a hospital staff that is sufficiently firm and supportive can "contain" the regressive features of an unstructured ward group. In such a setting the patient program may benefit from the mobilization of negative transference affects that gravitate to the surface and are subject to group transference interpretations (Boris 1973). These negative feelings then may not need to be acted on to sabotage other parts of the program.

Limit setting, as we have seen, is an important aspect of the borderline patient's treatment. When limit setting is too firm and is employed too rapidly and readily in a treatment program, the unfolding of the patient's psychopathology, both in action and in words, may be seriously impeded. Among the results of such an approach may be lost opportunities to understand the patient's fears, since they may not be permitted to emerge. On the other hand, when limit setting is so lax that patients can act out issues to a degree that frightens them, their increasing individual chaos can spread to the entire ward structure and involve other patients and staff. A major aspect of successful limit setting depends upon whether it is utilized as part of a caring, concerned, protective, and collaborative intervention with a patient or as a rejecting response and manifestation of countertransference hate.

## Therapist–Patient Issues in Hospital Treatment

If the therapist decides that hospitalization is indicated, a setting that allows him to continue regular appointments with his patient is crucial. The "abandoned child" theme, which emerges with intense rage and panic, remains among the major issues to be resolved. A hospital that encourages the therapist to continue with his patient during the hospitalization can offer the supportive structure in which this rage can be safely experienced and analyzed. For many borderline patients, hospitalization itself seems to threaten the loss of or abandonment by their therapist. The therapist's willingness to continue with the patient, in spite of the patient's conviction that he will be abandoned because of the dangerous, provocative behavior that necessitated hospitalization, also presents an opportunity for a new kind of experience.

A major aspect of the patient's hospital evaluation consists of the clarification of the patient's therapy, including the transference–countertransference issues. Under optimal circumstances the hospital unit can function as a consultant for the therapist and can clarify treatment issues to facilitate continuing work. The therapist who hospitalizes a regressed borderline patient may feel devalued, defensive, guilty, or ashamed as he relates to the hospital staff. In part these feelings are his countertransference responses to the patient's intense fury, devaluation, and projection of worthlessness, which the therapist may experience as a part of himself through projective identification. Earlier there may have been a reactivation in the therapist of primitive omnipotent and grandiose feelings, followed by shame for his supposed failure with the patient. When these countertransference feelings are coupled with the hospital staff's own omnipotent and grandiose responses, which include devaluation of the therapist and a wish to rescue the patient from him, the therapist and patient are placed in a situation that can accentuate the defensive splitting borderline patients tend to act out with any hospital staff. The experienced staff always keeps in mind its own propensity for certain countertransference responses to therapist and patient as it evaluates and treats the patient.

An important task for the hospital staff is the development of a safe environment in which the patient can experience and put into words his overwhelming feelings with his therapist. The borderline patient's readiness to use splitting as a defense can easily keep these feelings, especially anger, outside of the therapist's domain. The traditional use of separate therapists and administrators in many hospitals, both of whom are on the hospital staff, tends to support the splitting process in borderline patients. The patient may be angry at the administrator for decisions that limit his activities or privileges, and idealize the therapist as the caring person who would not allow such things to happen if he had the power. When the therapist is a member of the hospital staff, it is sometimes possible for him to be both administrator and therapist. If the therapist cannot assume both roles, he can, in collaboration with the administrator, ally himself with administrative decisions—assuming that he is consulted and agrees with them. He can present to the patient his agreement with the administrator, especially when the patient attempts to avoid his anger with the therapist by devaluing the administrator for some management decision.

The hospital staff that excludes the outside or staff therapist from collaborative work with treatment planning may foster a continuation of pathological splitting and lose an opportunity to help the patient develop the capacity to love and hate the same person, an obviously important step in emotional growth. It also tends to perpetuate the unit's devaluation of the therapist and his work with the patient and further intensifies another aspect of the splitting process: The patient views the therapist as weak and worthless and idealizes the hospital or hospital administrator as the omnipotent, rescuing parent. The borderline patient's defensive use of splitting is supported whether the therapist is idealized or devalued; the hospital is then less able to help the patient and his therapist continue the work of reconciling murderous fury toward a therapist who is felt as an abandoning as well as a beloved, caring, holding parent.

Of course the hospital administration can only work collaboratively with a therapist if its assessment of the therapist's work is largely positive. Often the process of evaluation helps the therapist clarify issues for himself. Sometimes the staff can formulate issues that help the therapist think through countertransference difficulties that were interfering with therapy. Such countertransference issues that can be clarified through staff consultation usually are not deeply rooted psychopathological problems in the therapist but, rather, transient, overwhelming countertransference feelings that emerge in the heat of the treatment of regressed borderline patients. The hospital setting that protects the patient and takes the pressure off the survival issues in therapy often automatically allows the therapist to get his own perspective on countertransference issues. Sometimes a supportive, tactful consultation by an appropriate staff member helps complete the outside therapist's understanding of his work with his patient and helps him resume a useful therapeutic stance that focuses on the issues formulated.

How does the hospital staff proceed when it feels that there are serious, perhaps unresolvable difficulties in the therapist's work with his patient? The staff's obligation to the therapist and patient includes a careful assessment of its own possible devaluing countertransference responses to the therapist as part of the already defined splitting processes. When the staff feels increasingly certain that pathological countertransference difficulties exist that cannot be modified through consultation, it must carefully review the data obtained from patient and family and the therapist's work as presented in conferences and consultations that are tactful and supportive of him. The staff may, after this review, feel that countertransference difficulties or empathic failures based on limitations in the therapist's personality have led to an unresolvable impasse. This impasse, which may itself threaten the life of the patient, often is the major manifestation of countertransference hate that remains unmodified and largely unconscious. At such times the staff has little choice but to help the patient and therapist end their work. Goals then include (1) protecting the patient while helping him understand that there is an impasse and that he need not see this impasse in terms of his own badness or failure, and (2) helping the therapist maintain his self-esteem in the termination process while also helping him learn from that process. Ideally both patient and therapist should be supported to learn as much as possible, maintain their self-esteem, and say good-bye appropriately.

## Staff Countertransference Issues within the Hospital Milieu

The borderline patient presents special challenges to any hospital staff. His use of primitive defenses—projection, projective identification, and splitting—becomes especially manifest during the regression that leads to hospitalization, and may quickly involve the hospital staff (Main 1957). Some staff members may become recipients of aspects of the patient's projected positive, previously internalized self and object representations, while negative self and object representations are projected onto other staff members. This description is not meant in a literal sense but, rather, as a way of conceptualizing the intense, confusing affects and fantasies in the patient and staff. Often these projections coincide with similar but repressed affects, fantasies, and self and object representations in specific staff members. These staff members may have achieved much higher levels of integration and maturity; however, primitive aspects that were repressed can readily become reactivated in work with borderline patients, most of whom intuitively choose a staff member to project aspects of themselves that reverberate with similar but repressed aspects in that staff member. When these projected aspects are projective identifications, the patient's need then to control the staff member, and the latter's countertransference need to control the patient, compound the chaos of the splitting phenomena. The disagreements, fury, and often totally opposite views and fantasies staff members have about a specific borderline patient are manifestations of the splitting and projective identification process.

The implications of projective identification and splitting are profound. Staff members who are the recipients of cruel, punishing parts of the patient will tend to react to the patient in a cruel, sadistic, and punishing manner. Staff members who have received loving, idealized projected parts of the patient will tend to respond to him with a protective, parental love. Obviously a clash can occur between these two groups of staff members. These mechanisms also help to explain why different staff members may see the same patient in very different ways.

People who usually function at a high level of integration can feel and act in regressive ways in group settings, especially when there is a lack of structure or a breakdown in the group task. This observation is consistent with the experience of staff members in the hospital setting, who tend to act empathically on projections they receive from patients. Because patients can project different parts onto different staff members, an internal drama within the patient can become a battleground for the staff. Staff members can begin to act toward one another as if each one of them had the only correct view of the patient and as if the part the patient projected onto the other staff members were the only true part of those staff members.

A brief vignette illustrates aspects of these complex mechanisms of patient-staff interaction. At a staff meeting a series of angry outbursts occurred among nurses, social workers, and occupational therapists about who would be responsible for supervising cleaning up after a family night (which involved dinner and a discussion group for patients, their families, and staff members). Repeated accusations and recriminations centered around the feelings of each discipline that the others really did not care about them and did not really understand the burden of work they had, especially on the day that family night occurred. Interpretations of the personal problems of staff members began to appear. The heated discussion ultimately led to a detailed account about the specifics of clean-up.

It then became apparent that although the patients had agreed to assume responsibility for the preparation of food, serving, and clean-up, they tended to disappear during the day and after the meeting, leaving much of the actual preparation and clean-up to the staff. Instead of supervising, staff members were cooking and scrubbing pots. It became clearer that the staff members were fighting with one another while forgetting the origin of their problems, that is, their difficulties in working with the patients. The patients were not expressing any direct anger about their reluctance to fulfill their agreed-upon participation in family night and their simultaneous wish to be cared for and fed by the staff. In its meeting the staff was oblivious to this reality. Instead they showed massive anger toward one another for not caring or doing enough for one another.

Another aspect of the staff's countertransference difficulties with borderline patients involves a process in which the patient is labeled as "manipulative." Manipulation for many borderline patients is largely unconscious and characterological, has important adaptive elements, and helps keep some of them from feeling and being totally alone. When the patient, however, is seen predominantly as a conscious, deliberate manipulator in the negative sense, the staff feels entitled to make unrealistic demands, punish the patient, and even threaten him with discharge (Hartocollis 1972). An observer who is not part of this ward process is often impressed with the almost total lack of empathy for the patient's pain or distress. It is as if the patient had succeeded in convincing the staff that only his negative aspects exist; at such times the staff may find it impossible to see any other part.

As stated, borderline patients use manipulation in their relations with people. Their primitive narcissism, which is part of their entitlement to survive, and the neediness associated with it, as well as the voracious oral quality of their hunger and rage, are often accompanied by a manipulative attitude when this neediness is most manifest. To miss the patient's pain, desperation, and distress, however, is to allow the splitting and projective identifications to become the staff's only view of the patient. This image of the patient as manipulator is also evidence of the patient's success in getting himself punished and devalued, a process that may involve projections of his primitive, archaic superego. Often the patient is seen by the staff as manipulative when he is most suicidal and desperate. At these times staff countertransference hate is potentially lethal (Maltsberger and Buie 1974).

A hospital staff working with borderline patients has the responsibility to itself and its patients to be alert to the described countertransference danger signals. There is no simple prescription or solution for them. Obviously, the quality of the professional staff, in particular, their achievement of higher levels of ego functioning and a solid capacity for object relations without ready utilization of primitive projective defenses, is important. In spite of the maturity of the staff, however, regressive group phenomena, especially in work with borderline patients, are inevitable (Hartocollis 1972).

The structure of the hospital unit becomes important in the resolution of these regressive staff responses. Regular staff meetings at which patient and patient–staff issues are open to scrutiny in a nonthreatening environment are particularly useful. Staff members who know each other well are less likely to respond regressively to a borderline patient's projections, that is, staff members' reality-testing capacities are enhanced when they have prolonged contact with other staff members in settings where they can learn clearly the reliable, consistent responses and personality characteristics of their co-workers.

A hospital administrative hierarchy that values the varying contributions of different disciplines and workers and clearly defines staff responsibilities and skills aids in minimizing projections. Such an administration also understands the importance of establishing sufficient task-oriented groups for both patient and staff needs to protect against a staff regressive pull (Garza-Guerrero 1975). The ability of the hospital or unit director to maintain equanimity in the face of the regressive propensities of staff and patients may be a crucial ingredient in successful hospital treatment. The administrator who respects staff and patients, who can tolerate their anger without retaliating and yet be firm when necessary, and who can delegate power unambivalently can provide the mature "holding environment" and a model for identification for the staff that facilitates a similar experience for the patients.

---------------------------Twelve---------------------------

# Treatment of
# the Aggressive Acting-Out
# Patient

As concern grows about problems of violence, crime, delin-
quency, and serious drug abuse in our society, questions
about therapeutic approaches have recently received increasing attention. Group and family therapy, encounter
groups, halfway houses, therapeutic communities, and
operant conditioning methods have been described as
exciting and promising treatment possibilities.

Understandably, individual psychotherapy has not been
viewed as a method that has much to offer such a large
patient population when limited human resources are already
overburdened with seemingly insoluble treatment tasks.
Still, the individual psychotherapeutic approach can be
extremely useful (1) in defining the therapeutic issues that
any treatment modality involving these patients has to face,
(2) in studying the countertransference problems that most

workers will experience with these patients, and (3) in improving individual psychotherapeutic techniques for the treatment of adolescent, psychotic, and borderline patients who manifest certain elements of the problem that patients with more severe aggressive, acting-out character disorders present in pure culture. In addition, individual treatment of selected patients in this group can be a rewarding experience for both participants. In this chapter I shall focus on some issues involved in treating aggressive acting-out patients, and stress transference and countertransference problems.

Although different in many ways, severely aggressive acting-out patients share certain characteristics: an inability to tolerate frustration and delay, major conflicts involving oral ambivalence, serious problems with trusting, a tendency to assume a paranoid position or at least to externalize responsibility, a poor capacity to form a working alliance with another person, and little capacity for self-observation. Their frightening anger can be hidden by such primitive defenses as denial, distortion, projection, reaction formation, and hypochondriasis, or, most frequently, by flight, literally or through drugs, from the situation causing their rage.

Engaging these patients in treatment can be a difficult task, because their usual flight mechanisms may keep them from returning for their next appointment. The therapist's ability to interest the patient in looking at himself, defining "problems" instead of allowing him to present himself as totally bad, and early emphasis on the trust problem are important ingredients in the preliminary work with these patients. The personality, conflicts, and skills of the therapist will be a major factor in determining his success in working with these patients. I shall discuss these aspects of the therapist as they apply to several issues in the treatment of this group of patients.

## Violence and Aggressiveness

The core conflict of most of these patients involves the persistence of, or regression to, the infantile devour-or-be-devoured position, although their higher-level defenses may mask this conflict. Wishes for closeness and nurturance either lead to the terror of engulfment and fusion, or to inevitable frustration of their feelings of entitlement to be nourished, followed by the primitive rage of the small child. What is frightening in this group is that the primitive fury is now present in a patient with an adult body capable of real destruction. And some of these patients are seen by us after they have put this destructive fury into action. Realistically, then, they can pose a threat to a person who wants to work with them.

Although there are situations in which work with such patients presents a genuine danger for the therapist or potential therapist, the threat is more often a feeling of inner terror in the therapist derived from his own conflicts. This feeling is often projected onto his patient, adding to the patient's fear of impending loss of control. The therapist in this situation does two things: (1) He may communicate his own difficulties with his own aggression to the patient, and (2) he may act in such a way that he places the patient in a bind that leads either to flight or to the possibility of some violent outburst toward the therapist.

The therapist's inability to convey the feeling of stability and confidence in which successful treatment can occur is compounded by his need to get rid of his own violent impulses stirred up by the patient by putting them onto the patient, who intuitively senses the therapist's difficulties. On some level the therapist may be aware that he is doing this, or he may only be aware that he wants to rescue the patient. He therefore may withdraw emotionally and lose his patient, or overcompensate by placing himself in a situation that is realistically dangerous—for example, forcing himself on a patient overwhelmed by wishes and fears of fusion or aggressively out of control.

There is a fine line between appropriately firm, confident intervention with a frightened patient and a smothering imposition by the therapist that can lead to serious consequences. However, one can usually count on the flight mechanisms of this group of patients to minimize the risks to the therapist when he makes a mistake. In my experience as therapist and supervisor with this group of patients inside and outside of prisons, only several potentially serious incidents have occurred, all related to some variety of the inappropriate type of intervention described.

Most members of this group of patients have serious difficulty in distinguishing their murderous fantasies from reality. And because their ego boundaries are often ill defined, they are not clear as to whether they have really hurt someone, or whether someone is about to hurt them. In addition, these patients often actually live in a dangerous, distrustful environment; it may be impossible for the therapist to separate in his own mind the intrapsychic conflict of the patient from the dangers in the patient's real world. In some extreme circumstances several patients became treatable in prison only when they were in maximum security isolation, so that the external environment became safe for the moment.

One of the therapeutic tasks with these patients is the repeated differentiation of fantasy from reality, and inner from outer. The therapist who has a major tendency to regress in similar but less marked ways when confronted with his or the patient's anger under stress will have obvious difficulty. Rather than maintaining an empathic capacity to grasp the patient's distress and be in touch with his inner terror as well as real present and past deprivation, the therapist may respond to the patient's life-and-death feelings as if they were too real. The result may be a loss of empathy, including withdrawal, attack, or the described overbearing rescue, which may cause the patient to resort to his usual flight mechanisms.

The effective therapist is comfortable with his own anger. He is aware of it, can tolerate it without projecting it, can test how much really belongs to the patient, and does not lose this ability when faced with a frightened and frightening patient who never had that capacity or who has lost it. No therapist exists who has this ability all the time. We depend on the therapist's strength most of the time to be able to test the reality of the fantasies aroused in him by these patients and distinguish his feelings from theirs, and to endure in the face of his own and the patient's anxieties. Included is his ability to distinguish fantasies from real dangers to himself or the patient as he works with him. When the therapist decides that real dangers exist for himself, he must define the limits in which he can work with the patient.

## Limit Setting

I want to discuss three aspects of limit setting: its meanings to the patient, the limits necessary that may make therapy possible, and the definition of who the therapist is and what he can tolerate as a human being.

Many of these patients have had backgrounds of deprivation and neglect. Their feelings of abandonment are often based on real experiences of parents or parent surrogates not caring for or abandoning them. Their childhoods have included experiences of not being able to depend on their parents to protect them or comfort them. Translating such experiences into the issues that arise in therapy with these patients, nonintervention when the patient is out of control or realistically perceives that he is losing control can easily be interpreted by such a patient as evidence that the therapist does not care. At the same time, however, intervention, for instance, prohibiting a specific piece of behavior, is often viewed by therapists as an interference with the autonomy of the patient and as the elimination of choices the patient has.

Any limit setting intervention does ultimately extract a price the therapist has to pay later—for example, arousing omnipotent fantasies about the therapist that have to be resolved in future treatment. But without the intervention, therapy may be impossible, for the patient frequently does not have the choices ascribed to him. Instead, he often can only repeat earlier patterns: to flee instead of acting impulsively, or to put an aggressive, destructive fantasy into action. If the therapist chooses not to intervene, he risks losing the patient, who may have no choice but to view the therapist as the same as his noncaring, nonprotective parents.

The therapist's judgment is crucial if the intervention is to be successful. If the therapist's assessment that the patient is out of control is correct, his limit setting action can be a new experience for the patient with a person who appropriately cares and protects, as we have already seen. In contrast, if the therapist has intervened because of his own conflicts and need to project anxiety and anger onto the patient, he can lose his patient by compromising the patient's tenuous capacity to function autonomously. The patient may then leave treatment feeling controlled and smothered.

Limit setting at times may include involving a probation or parole officer or the police when the therapist feels the dangers of the situation for the patient warrant it. The judgment of the therapist here is particularly crucial for the future of any treatment. The result can be a grateful patient with an increasing capacity to maintain a working relationship, or a furious former patient who justifiably feels betrayed. The task can be easier when the patient is willing to be involved in weighing the evidence for the intervention. But when a patient is out of control, such ego strength may not be evident.

Sometimes the therapist sets limits in part because the patient is in distress, but also because the patient's behavior goes beyond the limits that the therapist can tolerate personally. For example, a patient who has made repeated homicidal threats can cause the therapist so much distress that he forbids the patient to possess any dangerous weapons as a condition for continued treatment. Obviously, such a position by the therapist protects the patient from making a fatal mistake, but the primary motivation at the time the therapist makes such a decision may be his own incapacity to tolerate such anxiety-arousing and potentially self-destructive behavior on the part of the patient. In addition, such an intervention has implications in whether the patient perceives it also as a caring gesture or as an incapacity of the therapist to tolerate what is necessary in working with him. Some of these theoretical and clinical issues are illustrated in the following vignette.

## Clinical Illustration

The patient was a 24-year-old single man who began treatment in prison six weeks before his scheduled parole hearing. He had been in the prison for several years for assault and battery during an armed robbery; four years before his present offense, he had been found guilty of manslaughter in a car accident in which three friends had died. The evaluation staff was unclear why he had applied for treatment, but observed that he was frightened and belligerent. They wondered if he sensed his anxiety about his parole hearing and hoped that the treatment unit would intervene.

His history revealed that he came from a middle-class family with a veneer of stability. His parents had almost divorced several times, however, and although they lived together, they had not talked to each other for years. His mother drank excessively at times and was known to have had extramarital affairs. The patient described his father as strict and punitive, moody and sulky, spending as much time away from home as he could.

The patient had an older brother and sister; he was particularly close to his sister, whom he described as very much like himself. She had to be transferred from a mental hospital because of her unmanageable behavior. He and his sister each had made several suicide attempts, the patient's last occurring in his jail cell, after the car accident, when he attempted to hang himself.

Few data are available about the patient's early years, except that he was born with a harelip that was repaired in infancy. In school he made the honor roll until the ninth grade, when his behavior began to deteriorate. From the age of 16 to his present sentence, he was arrested 13 times and was convicted of auto violations, drunkenness, disturbing the peace, breaking and entering, larceny, and the described manslaughter and assault. He had served four previous brief prison sentences.

In the first few sessions with his therapist, the patient spelled out his impulsivity and fears of going crazy or out of control. He stated that he had fears of running wild in the prison, screaming, or smashing things; he controlled these feelings by going to his cell and staying by himself. He described his history of difficulties with the law and outlined that his seven months out of prison after the manslaughter conviction were successful until he met the mother of one of the friends killed in the auto accident:

> She looked at me and I fell apart and drank, and in three hours was picked up. . . . How did I feel? I killed her son. I was panicky and had to get away. I can't go home because I can't stand people who remind me of this. . . . When people become emotionally involved with me I hurt them, and when people try to help me I fail them. . . . I hate authority. I got this from my father. I used to hate him; now I feel I have no relationship with him. I'm worried whether I'm a stable person.

One of the issues the therapist discussed with the patient was the treatment unit's policy of writing a letter to the parole board stating the therapist's thoughts about the patient and any information that might be useful to the board in its deliberations. Clearly such a letter brought issues of trust and confidentiality to the surface; at its best the parole letter could be used as a collaborative effort between patient and therapist. In preparing to discuss the writing of this letter with the patient, the therapist became aware of his own fantasies that any limit setting recommendation would arouse the patient's fury and lead to the patient's leaving treatment or even physically assaulting the therapist. In spite of these fantasies and fears, the therapist felt he had sufficient evidence to suggest in his letter that the patient was not ready for parole. Because he could not get the patient's collaboration in writing the letter, he presented a draft to the patient. One portion read: "This inmate in the past has been subject to impulsive destructive acts, and although he has recently been making some attempts at socialization and control of this tendency, it is my opinion that the gains have not been sufficient to enable him to modify his behavior, should he be faced with stresses similar to those he has been subjected to in the past." Instead of the indignation and fury the therapist expected, the patient's only comment was that the "destructive acts" be changed to "destructive acts against himself"; the therapist agreed to this.

In the following session the patient talked about his problem with distrust of the therapist and expressed surprise that he had accepted the therapist's letter with only mild anger. He missed the next appointment because of his parole board hearing. He returned the following week, quiet and angry. "I'm in a bitchy mood. I feel lousy. I got my parole." The therapist asked how he felt about it. He could hardly reply, getting up from his chair and checking the closet to see if a tape recorder was hidden. "The administration is fooling you too and has it there without your knowledge." Later he said, "It was a terrible hearing. I only spoke for 30 seconds. At least I didn't have a chance to talk myself out of the parole."

What there was of a working relationship continued to deteriorate after this meeting. Distrust markedly increased, the patient having increasing difficulty saying anything to the therapist. He spoke of his brother, who would lead him into things and then skip out. He wondered how many years of training the therapist had had and whether he was still a student. The patient came for several more interviews but, in spite of considerable efforts by his therapist, broke off treatment several weeks before being paroled.

This vignette illustrates the struggles of a therapist who seems to have made a correct assessment of the patient's tenuous capacity to control his impulses in spite of the therapist's conscious countertransference fantasies about the dangers of setting limits. It also spells out the meaning to the patient of the parole board's decision to release him. He viewed this action as a confirmation that the therapist was uncaring and helpless; in that setting he became extremely distrustful, used increasing projection, and felt that the therapist had abandoned him. The therapist could find no way to reestablish any working relationship, and, as is characteristic of such patients, this one quickly gave up treatment.

## The Therapist as a Real Person

Limit setting is part of the process of a therapist's defining who he is, what he can tolerate, how he himself responds to stress, and whether he really cares about his patient. This definition of the therapist as a real person is often a crucial ingredient in successful therapy with these patients.

There are specific reasons why this group of patients requires much more than a mirrorlike therapist. Because these patients usually have significant ego defects, major changes that may occur through psychotherapy include identifications with certain aspects of the therapist, which must be clearly visible. Before a relationship can be established that can lead to a process of identification, the patient has to see the therapist as he really is, not as a confirmation of all his negative cultural expectations as well as his projections and distortions. A nondirective therapist permits these problems to occur in a group of patients all too prone to lose the capacity for testing reality.

The problems arising when therapists from one cultural background attempt to work with patients from a very different life experience are enormous. The honesty and integrity of the therapist and his willingness to reveal his position, knowledge, or lack of it can cut through the cultural differences, provided the therapist is genuine in his stance. Particularly for adolescent patients, a real therapist willing to stand for real values and not attack, provoke, or run away himself is a new kind of experience.

The therapist who wants to help such patients with their murderous rage, and yet who recognizes their need for an experience with a real person, faces a genuine dilemma. In order to tolerate their anger and not be destroyed by it, he must seemingly adopt an omnipotent position very different from that of a "real" person vulnerable to feeling hurt by such fury and hate. Yet it is also crucial that the therapist *be* a real person with human qualities, so that the patient can have a clearer picture of him as a model for identification. This real aspect of the therapist also helps the patient evaluate the reality of his fantasies about his therapist. The capable therapist with these patients is one who can assume both positions flexibly, and in rapid succession when necessary. Both positions involve new experiences, one concerning whether angry fantasies destroy and drive important people away, the other concerning a real person who cares what the patient believes and who is willing to let the patient know what he stands for.

## Containment

Winnicott's (1965) concepts of the "holding environment" and "good-enough mothering," although coming from mother–child observation and utilizing a different theoretical framework, are closely related to Kohut's concept of the "selfobject." Like Kohut, he defines a dyadic relationship in which an environment of safety, security, and trust is created that allows the child (or patient) to feel "held" and complete. In such an environment, deficiencies can momentarily be complemented by the other person in the dyad. Growth potential can be reactivated, and unresolved issues can be settled.

Borderline patients talk vividly about their longings to be held and contained, and their panic about being dropped, abandoned, and rejected. Some primitive people engage in criminal acts in order to provoke the correctional system into providing the containment they need but that is not within their capacities to find elsewhere. Correctional workers all know of examples of poorly executed antisocial activity that can best be explained as the acted-out wish and need to be caught and protected (and sometimes punished as well). The containment that the correctional system offers provides functions that are absent, either transiently or permanently, in offenders with borderline and narcissistic personality features. These containment or holding functions are similar to the selfobject functions a therapist provides in a treatment setting. Containment also provides the necessary controls for offenders who have ego defects related to impulse control. Rather than serving as a negative or punitive use of force, the containment function of the correctional system can provide the beginnings of an effective treatment program that can address the specific defects or deficiencies of people who become a part of it.

An effective holding treatment program for an individual with impulse control difficulties can provide a safe environment that will allow him to talk about the issues in his past and present. It is not unusual for the individual to blame the correctional system for his difficulties and resent his containment and the fact that he is required to be in a treatment program. Once he realizes, however, that he does not have to assume responsibility for the dependency longings that the containment or holding can arouse, and begins to feel comfortable with the security that the containment provides, he will begin to respond in a variety of ways depending on his psychopathology, self-cohesiveness, and ego capacities. For some, the security of the new situation, which permits the formation of a relatively stable selfobject transference, enables them fairly quickly to experience and talk about the disappointments in their lives as well as in the treatment situation. With more primitive people, that is, those who are borderline or have a severe narcissistic personality disorder, the containment often begins with an initial period of anger, with use of projection as a major defense, during which the individual tests the security of the containment and the worker's capacity to bear his rage without rejection or punishment. Thus, the holding environment can provide a secure place for anger to be expressed in words by those people who need to experience that their anger will not destroy. The physical security available in correctional settings also helps to assure this safe expression of anger. In addition, such a setting sometimes makes it possible to sort out the individual's projections of anger from genuine dangers; that is, a maximum-security setting that precludes contact with other inmates not only can protect an individual from real dangers, but can also clarify that he may be using projection to avoid acknowledgment of his own anger. Finally, the holding environment protects against the wish to run away, which impulsive offenders are very likely to carry out, by providing the parental protective function that Mahler (1968) describes as necessary in the process of separation and individuation.

When the holding environment is established in non-correctional therapeutic settings, it can include individual and group therapy, but in the prison and parole environments, it becomes a much broader concept. The effective structuring of the environment for the impulsive person by the variety of personnel in the system—judge, administrator, mental health professional, probation or parole officer, correctional officer or shop foreman—not only provides containment, but also enables the formation of selfobject transferences with any number of these people. The fact that so many different personnel are available often gives the individual an opportunity to relate to someone of his choosing who can provide qualities he admires or who can respond to his need to be mirrored, understood, or validated. The appropriate responses from the prison staff are crucial in enabling growth to take place. Countertransference difficulties or failure to understand the needs of the specific person in the program can lead to a repetition of the experiences that led to his hopelessness, despair, and chronic feelings of betrayal.

In addition to feelings of overt sadism, caretakers can find themselves withdrawing and feeling disdainful and uninterested in the people they should be trying to understand and help. Because selfobject transferences can flourish only by means of understanding the individual's pain and anger from his own perspective, the countertransference reactions of the staff are more likely to repeat negative experiences with important people in his life than to allow the opportunity for a new experience that permits the growth and resolution of previous developmental arrests.

In order to provide the holding environment required by the individuals they wish to help, the caretakers themselves must have their own holding environment. Ideally, such an environment is established by the superintendent of an institution or the chief of a court clinic, parole, or probation program. A caring, respected leader who can be firm when necessary, without being punitive or retaliatory, provides an opportunity for the staff to use him as a selfobject who can be idealized to whatever degree is needed. The staff can also use the various clinical and administrative meetings to obtain the required amounts of mirroring, validating, and understanding from him and people working with him on a supervisory level. Under such circumstances the work setting can be a gratifying, creative experience for the staff.

# Thirteen

# Psychotherapy of Schizophrenia

## Semrad's Contributions

Psychiatric residents coming to Boston for their training usually had no difficulty finding excellent supervisors who encouraged them to work with primitive patients and to read the basic papers of therapists who had struggled themselves with these patients. But anyone who worked as a psychiatric resident at the Massachusetts Mental Health Center would have had one major influence—Elvin Semrad. Semrad was a unique figure in American psychiatry. His influence in Boston was profound, largely based upon the impact of his clinical teaching, which included interviews of patients in the presence of staff. Because he published relatively little, his work is known by few people outside Boston who are not students of the psychoanalytic psychotherapeutic approach to schizophrenics. But in Boston, Semrad was a figure that a trainee would have had to struggle with, or against, as he tried to learn and ultimately define what came from Semrad, from his other teachers, and from himself. This process often occurred with significant personal pain, despair, envy, and also, for many, satisfaction.

To integrate Semrad's contributions with some of the recent work of other clinicians and theoreticians, I shall first define Elvin Semrad's clinical stance, style, and theoretical framework. Perhaps one of Semrad's contributions was that as a "natural" he transcended all frameworks while using aspects of many. By calling him a "natural," I mean that Semrad had an intuitive, empathic gift that he used to contact and sustain people in a clinical situation while he focused on their emotional pain. This capacity, which Semrad implied required much personal work to develop, cut through all theoretical frameworks.

Here are some of the major tenets of Semrad's approach (Semrad 1954, 1969; Khantzian, Dalsimer, and Semrad 1969):

1. Semrad's interviews demonstrated that support through empathic understanding of another person's pain can very often permit a withdrawn or confused schizophrenic to make affective contact with another person, although that contact might exist only for part of an interview.

2. With adequate support and an empathic sharing of emotional pain, the patient's psychosis could be profoundly altered, at least during the moments of that empathic contact; that is, schizophrenic disorganization coexists only with difficulty with an empathic human relationship that adequately supports.

3. The schizophrenic's decompensation often occurs secondary to loss, real or fantasied. Supportively helping the person bear that loss counteracts the

schizophrenic avoidance devices. These devices can also be viewed as part of the regression that occurs with the schizophrenic's inability to bear sadness as well as the rage following the loss or disappointment. The therapist's support allows the sadness to be borne, permitting a mourning process to occur in which the individual "acknowledges, bears, and puts into perspective" the painful reality. Once the person has carried out this process or has the capacity to carry out this process by himself (that is, to mourn or bear sadness), the person is no longer schizophrenic. Before he can reach that point, he also has to put his rage into perspective and learn that it does not have to destroy.

4. Part of the process of helping the schizophrenic patient address his avoidance devices and his helplessness is an approach that stresses the patient's responsibility for his dilemma. Semrad asking a confused schizophrenic how he "arranged it for himself to come to the hospital" is a classic example.

5. Good treatment of schizophrenia requires optimal support and optimal frustration. This is what Semrad called "giving with one hand and taking away with the other."

6. Schizophrenics in particular have difficulty integrating affects. They tend to avoid acknowledging what they have felt, or partially acknowledge it by attempting to keep it separate from the awareness of the bodily feeling that is a component of that affect and that is often a part of an unassimilated introject. Semrad's style—the "tour of the body," asking a patient, organ by organ, exactly where he experienced a feeling—was directed toward helping the patient become aware of a feeling and its bodily

components, in part as an aid in learning to acknowledge and bear uncomfortable, but human, feelings.

7. The avoidance devices of schizophrenics make them vague and unclear about specific events and feelings; much of the psychotherapeutic work includes the support and persistence of the therapist in assisting the patient to spell out the details of what he does not want to think or talk about or look at.

8. Successful treatment occurs when the therapist, who has transiently become a substitute for the lost object, is no longer necessary because those attributes of the therapist that the patient likes and needs have become a part of the patient. The schizophrenic patient remains vulnerable to the degree that this internalization process is incomplete.

This partial and oversimplified statement of Semrad's therapeutic stance does not capture the excitement of observing one human being's caring wish to help another expressed with such seeming ease, simplicity, and effectiveness.

How, then, can we use Semrad's style and framework, and relate them to some other major theoretical and clinical frameworks, in a way that can add further clarity to aspects of clinical work with schizophrenics?

Several frames of reference that have much in common with Semrad's clinical style are useful in defining the establishment of a safe, trusting environment that allows the patient sufficient comfort, sustenance, and gratification to make the therapeutic work possible. Winnicott's (1965) "holding environment" concepts and Kohut's (1971, 1977) concepts of narcissistic or "selfobject" transferences are particularly applicable to work with schizophrenic patients, although these concepts have been described in the literature more often in defining treatment issues with borderline and narcissistic personality disorders. Indeed, I believe that many schizophrenics have a vulnerability, present before their decompensation, that leaves them functioning somewhere in the sphere of patients defined as having borderline or narcissistic personalities.

Many schizophrenics function effectively before the onset of their psychosis in part because they have a relationship with someone that provides the selfobject qualities they require. When that relationship is lost, the severe fragmentation of the self that is characteristic of the schizophrenic process occurs. The psychotherapeutic approach to the schizophrenic requires a setting in which the therapist helps the patient reestablish the narcissistic transferences that sustained him in the past. After the onset of schizophrenia, these narcissistic or selfobject transferences are often lower on the developmental scale and involve more merger and fusion when compared with the premorbid primitive transferences, with their somewhat greater self and object differentiation. The therapist's empathic understanding of the selfobject role he serves in these transferences, as well as his grasp of the patient's distrust, vulnerabilities, pain, disorganization, and other specific needs and fears, helps create the necessary therapeutic setting. The awareness that the schizophrenic has an exquisite tendency to fragment and retreat to more primitive defenses and styles of relating provides the therapist with the empathic framework in which he can decide how much support, silence, activity, clarification, or interpretation is appropriate and necessary from moment to moment and session to session. Semrad's empathic style provided the support and holding that allowed the spectrum of narcissistic or selfobject transferences to unfold, if only at first during the interview with him. The experience for the patient (as well as for the observers in the room during an interview with the patient) was one of being enclosed in a warm matrix while some of the most painful feelings and experiences of a person's life were explored.

Winnicott's models of the holding environment and good-enough mothering complement Kohut's selfobject formulations. Winnicott described the vulnerabilities of primitive patients caused by failures of support and holding in childhood. These vulnerabilities derive from parental figures who were unable, for a variety of reasons, to respond adequately to the phase-specific needs of the growing child. The childhood failures in good-enough mothering and the holding environment in part account for the vulnerabilities in future schizophrenics. The therapeutic task in working with already schizophrenic patients consists in establishing an environment that provides the necessary support and holding. This holding environment includes the reestablishment of primitive selfobject transferences that allow a reliving of past disappointments and an exploration of recent losses and their manifestations in the transference.

The development of stable primitive transferences occurs only gradually; at first they appear transiently when the patient feels supported and understood. These momentary narcissistic or selfobject transferences dissolve at the point that affect, wish, impulse, longing, or fear overwhelms the patient's tenuous capacity to maintain the primitive transference. Because the schizophrenic patient has such a propensity to fragment, especially early in treatment, supportive approaches are essential. They also provide the patient with models that ultimately can be internalized; the result, in turn, is a greater capacity for the patient to form stable primitive transferences.

In therapeutic work with schizophrenics and in supervision of trainees working with them, techniques and principles that derive from Semrad's style can be usefully applied.

Many of them address the patient's defective ego capacities, terror of human relationships, helplessness, ambivalence, and confusion and provide what Semrad called a corrective ego experience.

## Decision-Making Deficiencies

An important aspect of a schizophrenic's difficulties is his inability to synthesize opposing aspects of himself, such as his many and conflicting self and object representations, while keeping inside and outside clearly defined. The incapacitating ambivalence described by Bleuler illustrates this process; it is an aspect of fragmentation and a lack of synthetic ego functioning. The catatonic stupor can be a manifestation of a terrifying indecision: To move can be linked with the urge to kill. Catatonia is thus the compromise that prevents destructiveness from occurring by keeping the patient in perpetual immobility.

The therapeutic position that focuses on the schizophrenic's difficulties in decision-making presents an approach in which the therapist's questions provide the model for weighing the factors that become part of a decision. The therapist in this process functions in part as an "auxiliary ego," using that synthesizing capacity that the patient lacks. The insight that indecision is itself a decision is a major step in this process; it also confronts the patient with his own responsibility for the position he is in. Semrad's question, "How did you arrange it for yourself?" illustrates this stance. The repeated clarification of the patient's confusion —how he intends to do something or get something he thinks he wants, and how he decided that he wanted something in the first place—supports this decision-making capacity, which can develop slowly over a long period of time.

# The Paradoxical Position

Weisman (1965) has stated that a major task in all psychotherapy is the unmasking of the paradoxes and contradictions in a person's feelings, fantasies, and beliefs. This approach is particularly useful in the psychotherapy of schizophrenia, because these patients have major difficulties with their contradictory and unintegrated self and object representations, contradictory fragments of a disorganized self, and beliefs that may totally disagree with other beliefs that they stated moments before. These paradoxes are supported by their uses of denial, projection, distortion, and splitting, which, in part, are their ways of not allowing themselves to think about or face their confusion.

A useful therapeutic stance can be one in which the therapist allows himself to become confused and shares his confusion with the patient. It can take the form of "I don't understand. First you have told me that this is the perfect job for you, and now you tell me that it's the worst possible job." The therapist, in this role, accomplishes certain specific functions: He confronts the avoidance devices by expecting details that the patient would rather not remember, he allows a useful projection to occur by feeling and expressing the patient's confusion, and he provides a model of someone with an ego capacity to bear and ultimately to synthesize contradictory affects, thoughts, experiences, and beliefs.

# Acknowledgment of the Fear before the Wish

A basic principle in most psychoanalytically oriented psychotherapy is that fears are examined before wishes. This approach is defined as part of defense analysis; it states that the patient must be comfortable with the meaning of his reluctance to talk about something before he can discuss the wishes or impulses behind the fear, shame, or guilt. In the psychotherapy of schizophrenia, this formulation is particularly important, because the schizophrenic is terrified of his own rage. This rage is often the unbearable affect that precipitated the schizophrenic regression, and is equated by the patient with murder and killing. To tell the confused schizophrenic that he is angry may be heard by him as a statement that he is a murderer. The exploration of his fears or guilt about his anger presents a way of allowing him to achieve the beginnings of some distance between himself and his terrifying impulses. At the height of the patient's terror over his rage, however, no statement about his anger, no matter how tactfully formulated, can be heard as anything but a statement about the patient as a murderer.

# Defining "Problems"

Because of the schizophrenic's fragmented self, loss of ego boundaries, inability to observe, and incapacity to see himself in anything but all-or-nothing terms, he can view himself only as totally bad or, when manically delusional, as totally perfect and omnipotent. The therapeutic stance that attempts to label the confusing material the patient presents, and to put this material into categories of problems, ultimately helps the patient develop precursors of the capacity to observe, maintain some distance from himself, define clearer ego boundaries, and gradually bear the complexities of his various feelings. Again, the patient has the therapist as a model for identification who can sort out the complexities of another human being's feelings without running, condemning, or rejecting.

## Responsibility Position

The therapist's expectation that the patient will assume responsibility for his past, present, and future has already been mentioned. Although the therapist can empathically respond to the fact that the patient has had real and painful disappointments in his past and is in a difficult and often seemingly hopeless current situation, he cannot allow the patient to seduce him from the stance that the patient has had and has a major responsibility for the genesis and solution of his problems. This position does not mean that the therapist loses his empathic sense that the patient can tolerate only a certain amount of confrontation about his responsibility. And he remembers the patient's need to feel the therapist's support as the patient faces his role in his life story and the resolution of the disorganizing pain in it.

It was Elvin Semrad's gift to be able to balance the patient's need for support with the human need for autonomy. A "natural" indeed.

# References

Balint, M. (1968). *The Basic Fault: Therapeutic Aspects of Regression*. London: Tavistock.

Bell, S. M. (1970). The development of the concept of object as related to infant-mother attachment. *Child Development* 41: 292–311.

Berkowitz, D. A. (1977). The vulnerability of the grandiose self and the psychology of acting-out patients. *International Review of Psycho-Analysis* 4:13–21.

Bibring, E. (1954). Psychoanalysis and the dynamic psycho-therapies. *Journal of the American Psychoanalytic Association* 2:745–770.

Bibring, G., Dwyer, T. F., Huntington, D. S., and Valenstein, A. F. (1961). A study of the psychological processes in pregnancy and of the earliest mother-child relationship: some propositions and currents. *Psychoanalytic Study of the Child* 16:9–72.

Bion, W. R. (1961). *Experiences in Groups and Other Papers*. New York: Basic Books.

Boris, H. N. (1973). Confrontation in the analysis of the transference resistance. In *Confrontation in Psychotherapy*, eds. G. Adler and P. G. Myerson, pp. 181–206. New York: Jason Aronson.

Boyer, L. B., and Giovacchini, P. L. (1967). *Psychoanalytic Treatment of Schizophrenia and Characterological Disorders.* New York: Science House.

Burnham, D. G., Gladstone, A. I., and Gibson, R. W. (1969). *Schizophrenia and the Need–Fear Dilemma.* New York: International Universities Press.

Chase, L. S., and Hire, A. W. (1966). Countertransference in the analysis of borderlines. Paper presented to the Boston Psychoanalytic Society and Institute, March 23.

Chessick, R. D. (1974). Defective ego feeling and the quest for being in the borderline patient. *International Journal of Psychoanalytic Psychotherapy* 3:73–89.

*Diagnostic and Statistical Manual of Mental Disorders*, Third Edition, (1980). Washington D.C.: American Psychiatric Association.

Erikson, E. H. (1959). *Identity and the Life Cycle.* New York: International Universities Press.

Fenichel, O. (1941). *Problems of Psychoanalytic Technique.* New York: Psychoanalytic Quarterly.

Fleming, J. (1972). Early object deprivation and transference phenomena: the working alliance. *Psychoanalytic Quarterly* 41:23–49.

——— (1975). Some observations on object constancy in the psychoanalysis of adults. *Journal of the American Psychoanalytic Association* 23:743–759.

Fraiberg, S. (1969). Libidinal object constancy and mental representation. *Psychoanalytic Study of the Child* 24:9–47.

Freud, A. (1936). *The Ego and the Mechanisms of Defense.* New York: International Universities Press, 1946.

——— (1954), Discussion of "The Widening Scope of Indications for Psychoanalysis," by L. Stone. *Journal of the American Psychoanalytic Association* 2:607–620.

Freud, S. (1909). Notes upon a case of obsessional neurosis. *Standard Edition* 10:153–318.

———— (1910a). The future prospects of psycho-analytic therapy. *Standard Edition* 11:139–151.

———— (1910b). "Wild" psychoanalysis. *Standard Edition* 11: 219–227.

———— (1912). The dynamics of transference. *Standard Edition* 12:99–108.

———— (1913). Further recommendations on the technique of psycho-analysis: on beginning the treatment. *Standard Edition* 12:122–144.

———— (1923). The ego and the id. *Standard Edition* 19:3–66.

———— (1937). Analysis terminable and interminable. *Standard Edition* 23:211–253.

Friedman, L. (1969). The therapeutic alliance. *International Journal of Psycho-Analysis* 50:139–153.

Frosch, J. (1964). The psychotic character: clinical psychiatric considerations. *Psychiatric Quarterly* 38:81–96.

———— (1967). Severe regressive states during analysis: summary. *Journal of the American Psychoanalytic Association* 15:606–625.

———— (1970). Psychoanalytic considerations of the psychotic character. *Journal of the American Psychoanalytic Association* 18:24–50.

Garza-Guerrero, A. C. (1975). Therapeutic uses of social subsystems in a hospital setting. *Journal of the National Association of Private Psychiatric Hospitals* 7:23–30.

Gedo, J., and Goldberg, A. (1973). *Models of the Mind*. Chicago: University of Chicago Press.

Gitelson, M. (1962). The curative factors in psycho-analysis: the first phase of psycho-analysis. *International Journal of Psycho-Analysis* 43:194–205.

Goldberg, A., ed. (1978). *The Psychology of the Self*. New York: International Universities Press.

Greenson, R. (1965). The working alliance and the transference neurosis. *Psychoanalytic Quarterly* 34:155–181.

Gunderson, J. G., and Kolb, J. E. (1978). Discriminating features of borderline patients. *American Journal of Psychiatry* 135: 792–796.

Gunderson, J. G., and Singer, M. T. (1975). Describing

borderline patients: an overview. *American Journal of Psychiatry* 132:1–10.

Guntrip, H. (1971). *Psychoanalytic Theory, Therapy and the Self.* New York: Basic Books.

Gutheil, T. G., and Havens, L. L. (1979). The therapeutic alliance: contemporary meanings and confusions. *International Review of Psycho-Analysis* 6:467–481.


Hartmann, H. (1939). *Ego Psychology and the Problem of Adaptation.* New York: International Universities Press, 1958.

Hartmann, H., and Loewenstein, R. M. (1962). Notes on the superego., *Psychoanalytic Study of the Child* 17:42–81.

Hartocollis, P. (1969). Young rebels in a mental hospital. *Bulletin of the Menninger Clinic* 33:215–232.

——— (1972). Aggressive behavior and the fear of violence. *Adolescence* 7:479–490.


Jacobson, E. (1957). Denial and repression. *Journal of the American Psychoanalytic Association* 5:81–92.

——— (1964). *The Self and the Object World.* New York: International Universities Press.


Kernberg, O. (1966). Structural derivatives of object relationships. *International Journal of Psycho-Analysis* 47:236–253.

——— (1967). Borderline personality organization. *Journal of the American Psychoanalytic Association* 15:641–685.

——— (1968). The treatment of patients with borderline personality organization. *International Journal of Psycho-Analysis* 49: 600–619.

——— (1973a). Psychoanalytic object relations theory, group processes, and administration: toward an integrative theory of hospital treatment. *Annual of Psychoanalysis* 1:363–388.

——— (1973b). Discussion of "Hospital Treatment of Borderline Patients" by G. Adler. *American Journal of Psychiatry* 130: 35–36.

———— (1975). *Borderline Conditions and Pathological Narcissism.* New York: Jason Aronson.

Khantzian, E. J., Dalsimer, J. S., and Semrad, E. V. (1969). The use of interpretation in the psychotherapy of schizophrenia. *American Journal of Psychotherapy* 23:182–197.

Kohut, H. (1968). The psychoanalytic treatment of narcissistic personality disorders. *Psychoanalytic Study of the Child* 23:86–113.

———— (1971). *The Analysis of the Self.* New York: International Universities Press.

———— (1977). *The Restoration of the Self.* New York: International Universities Press.

Kris, E. (1952). *Psychoanalytic Explorations of Art.* New York: International Universities Press.

Lewin, B. D. (1950). *The Psychoanalysis of Elation.* New York: W. W. Norton.

Lipton, S. D. (1977). The advantages of Freud's technique as shown in his analysis of the Rat Man. *International Journal of Psycho-Analysis* 58:255–273.

Little, M. (1960). On basic unity. *International Journal of Psycho-Analysis* 41:377–384.

———— (1966). Transference in borderline states. *International Journal of Psycho-Analysis* 47:476–485.

———— (1981). *Transference Neurosis and Transference Psychosis,* New York: Jason Aronson.

Loewald, H. W. (1962). Internalization, separation, mourning, and the superego. *Psychoanalytic Quarterly* 31:483–504.

Mahler, M. S. (1968). *On Human Symbiosis and the Vicissitudes of Individuation.* New York: International Universities Press.

Mahler, M. S., Furer, M., and Settlage, C. (1959). Severe emotional disturbances in childhood psychosis. *American Handbook of Psychiatry* 1:816–839.

Mahler, M. S., Pine, F., and Bergman, A. (1975). *The Psychological Birth of the Human Infant.* New York: Basic Books.

Main, T. F. (1957). The ailment. *British Journal of Medical Psychology* 30:129–145.

Maltsberger, J. T., and Buie, D. H. (1974). Countertransference hate in the treatment of suicidal patients. *Archives of General Psychiatry* 30:625–633.

——— (1980). The devices of suicide: revenge, riddance and rebirth. *International Review of Psycho-Analysis* 7:61–72.

Masterson, J. F. (1976). *Psychotherapy of the Borderline Adult.* New York: Brunner/Mazel.

Meissner, W. W. (1971). Notes on identification. II. Clarification of related concepts. *Psychoanalytic Quarterly* 40:277–302.

——— (1972). Notes on identification. III. The concept of identification. *Psychoanalytic Quarterly* 41:224–260.

——— (1978). *The Paranoid Process.* New York: Jason Aronson.

——— (1982). Notes on the potential differentiation of borderline conditions. *International Journal of Psychoanalytic Psychotherapy* 9:3–49.

Murray, J. M. (1964). Narcissism and the ego ideal. *Journal of the American Psychoanalytic Association* 12:477–528.

——— (1973). The purpose of confrontation. In *Confrontation in Psychotherapy*, ed. G. Adler and P. G. Myerson, pp. 49–66. New York: Jason Aronson.

Myerson, P. G. (1964). Discussion of "The Theory of Therapy in Relation to a Developmental Model of the Psychic Apparatus" by E. R. Zetzel. Paper presented to the Boston Psychoanalytic Society and Institute, January 22.

——— (1973). The meanings of confrontation. In *Confrontation in Psychotherapy*, ed. G. Adler and P. G. Myerson, pp. 21–38. New York: Jason Aronson.

——— (1976). The level of regression and the therapeutic work. Paper presented at the 11th Annual Tufts Symposium on Psychotherapy, Boston, April 9.

Ornstein, A. (1975). Discussion at the 11th Annual Tufts Symposium on Psychotherapy, Boston, April.

Perry, J. C., and Klerman, G. (1980). Clinical features of the borderline personality. *American Journal of Psychiatry* 137:165–173.

Piaget, J. (1937). *The Construction of Reality in the Child.* New York: Basic Books, 1967.

Rapaport, D. (1957). The theory of ego autonomy: a generalization. In *Collected Papers,* ed. M. M. Gill. New York: Basic Books, 1967.
———— (1967). A theoretical analysis of the superego concept. In *Collected Papers,* ed. M. M. Gill. New York: Basic Books.

Robertson, J., and Robertson, J. (1969). *John, Seventeen Months: For Nine Days in a Residential Nursery* (film). Britain: Concord Films Council; U.S.A.: New York University Films.
———— (1971). Young children in brief separation: a fresh look. *Psychoanalytic Study of the Child* 26:264–315.
Rosenfeld, H. A. (1965). *Psychotic States: A Psychoanalytic Approach.* New York: International Universities Press.

Sandler, J. (1960). On the concept of the superego. *Psychoanalytic Study of the Child* 15:128–162.
Sandler, J., and Rosenblatt, B. (1962). The concept of the representational world. *Psychoanalytic Study of the Child* 17:128–145.
Schafer, R. (1968). *Aspects of Internalization.* New York: International Universities Press.
Searles, H. F. (1963). Transference psychosis in the psychotherapy of chronic schizophrenia. *International Journal of Psycho-Analysis* 44:249–282.
Semrad, E. V. (1954). The treatment process. *American Journal of Psychiatry* 110:426–427.
———— (1968). Psychotherapy of the borderline patient. Paper presented at a conference at the Tufts University School of Medicine, Boston, April 4.
———— (1969). *Teaching Psychotherapy of Psychotic Patients.* New York: Grune & Stratton.
Shapiro, L. N. (1973). Confrontation with the "real" analyst. In *Confrontation in Psychotherapy,* ed. G. Adler and P. G. Myerson, pp. 207–224. New York: Jason Aronson.
Spitz, R. (1965). *The First Year of Life.* New York: International Universities Press.

Sterba, R. (1934). The fate of the ego in analytic therapy. *International Journal of Psycho-Analysis* 15:117–126.

Stone, L. (1961). *The Psychoanalytic Situation*. New York: International Universities Press.

Tolpin, M. (1971). On the beginnings of a cohesive self: an application of the concept of transmuting internalization to the study of the transitional object and signal anxiety. *Psychoanalytic Study of the Child* 26:316–352.

Vaillant, G. E. (1971). Theoretical hierarchy of adaptive ego mechanisms. *Archives of General Psychiatry* 24:107–118.

Volkan, V. D. (1976). *Primitive Internalized Object Relations*. New York: International Universities Press.

Weisman, A. (1965). *The Existential Core of Psychoanalysis: Reality Sense and Responsibility*. Boston: Little, Brown.

Winnicott, D. W. (1953). Transitional objects and transitional phenomena. In *Collected Papers*, pp. 229–242. London: Tavistock, 1958.

—— (1958). The capacity to be alone. In *The Maturational Processes and the Facilitating Environment*, pp. 29–36. New York: International Universities Press, 1965.

—— (1960). Ego distortion in terms of the true and false self. In *The Maturational Processes and the Facilitating Environment*, pp., 140–152. New York: International Universities Press, 1965.

—— (1965). *The Maturational Processes and the Facilitating Environment*. New York: International Universities Press.

—— (1969). The use of an object. *International Journal of Psycho-Analysis* 50:711–716.

Zetzel, E. R. (1956). The concept of transference. In *The Capacity for Emotional Growth*, pp. 168–181. New York: International Universities Press, 1970.

# Source Notes

"The Primary Basis of Borderline Psychopathology: Ambivalence or Insufficiency?" Adapted from "Definitive Treatment of the Borderline Personality" by Dan H. Buie and Gerald Adler. *International Journal of Psychoanalytic Psychotherapy* 9:51–87, 1982.

"Developmental Issues." Adapted from "Aloneness and Borderline Psychopathology: The Possible Relevance of Child Development Issues" by Gerald Adler and Dan H. Buie. *International Journal of Psycho-Analysis* 60:83–96, 1979; and "Definitive Treatment of the Borderline Personality" by Dan H. Buie and Gerald Adler. *International Journal of Psychoanalytic Psychotherapy* 9:51–87, 1982.

"Psychodynamics of Borderline Pathology." Adapted from "Aloneness and Borderline Psychopathology: The Possible Relevance of Child Development Issues" by Gerald Adler and Dan H. Buie. *International Journal of Psycho-Analysis* 60:83–96, 1979; and "Definitive Treatment of the Borderline Personality," by Dan H. Buie and Gerald Adler. *International Journal of Psychoanalytic Psychotherapy* 9:51–87, 1982.

"Treatment of the Primary Sector of Borderline Psychopathology." Adapted from "Aloneness and Borderline Psychopathology: The Possible Relevance of Child Development Issues" by Gerald Adler and Dan H. Buie. *International Journal of Psycho-Analysis* 60:83–96, 1979; and "Definitive Treatment of the Borderline Personality" by Dan H. Buie and Gerald Adler. *International Journal of Psychoanalytic Psychotherapy* 9:51–87, 1982.

"The Borderline–Narcissistic Personality Disorder Continuum." Adapted from "The Borderline–Narcissistic Personality Disorder Continuum" by Gerald Adler. *American Journal of Psychiatry* 138:46–50, 1981; and "Issues in the Treatment of the Borderline Patient" by Gerald Adler. In *Progress in Self Psychology*, ed. A. Goldberg and P. Stepansky, pp. 117–134. Hillsdale, N.J.: Erlbaum, 1984.

"The Myth of the Alliance." Adapted from "The Myth of the Alliance with Borderline Patients" by Gerald Adler. *American Journal of Psychiatry* 136:642–645, 1979; and "Transference, Real Relationship and Alliance" by Gerald Adler. *International Journal of Psycho-Analysis* 61:547–558, 1980.

"Uses of Confrontation." Adapted from "The Uses of Confrontation with Borderline Patients" by Dan H. Buie and Gerald Adler. *International Journal of Psychoanalytic Psychotherapy* 1:90–108, 1972.

"Misuses of Confrontation." Adapted from "The Misuses of Confrontation with Borderline Patients" by Gerald Adler and Dan H. Buie. *International Journal of Psychoanalytic Psychotherapy* 1:109–120, 1972.

"Regression in Psychotherapy: Disruptive or Therapeutic?" Adapted from "Regression in Psychotherapy: Disruptive or Therapeutic?" by Gerald Adler. *International Journal of Psychoanalytic Psychotherapy* 3:252–264, 1974.

"Devaluation and Countertransference." Adapted from "Valuing and Devaluing in the Psychotherapeutic Process" by Gerald Adler. *Archives of General Psychiatry* 22:454–461, copyright 1970, American Medical Association, 1970; "Helplessness in the Helpers" by Gerald Alder. *British Journal of Medical Psychology* 45:315–326, 1972; and "Issues in the Treatment of the Borderline Patient" by Gerald Adler. In *Kohut's Legacy: Contributions to Self*

*Psychology*, ed. P. E. Stepansky and A. Goldberg, pp. 117–134. Hillsdale, N.J.: The Analytic Press, 1984.

"Hospital Management." Adapted from "Hospital Management of Borderline Patients" by Gerald Adler. In *Borderline Personality Disorders: The Concept, the Syndrome, the Patient*, ed. P. Hartocollis, pp. 307–323. New York: International Universities Press, 1977; and "Hospital Treatment of Borderline Patients" by Gerald Adler. *American Journal of Psychiatry* 130:32–36, 1973.

"Treatment of the Aggressive Acting-Out Patient." Adapted from "Some Difficulties in the Treatment of the Aggressive Acting-Out Patient" by Gerald Adler and Leon N. Shapiro. *American Journal of Psychotherapy* 27:548–556, 1973; and "Recent Psychoanalytic Contributions to the Understanding and Treatment of Criminal Behaviour" by Gerald Adler. *International Journal of Offender Therapy and Comparative Criminology* 26:281–287, 1982.

"Psychotherapy of Schizophrenia: Semrad's Contributions." Adapted from "The Psychotherapy of Schizophrenia: Semrad's Contributions to Current Psychoanalytic Concepts" by Gerald Adler. *Schizophrenia Bulletin* 5:130–137, 1979.

# Index